MW01196499

BOOKS BY NNEKA UNACHUKWU, M.D

The EntreMD Method

Made for More

The Visibility Formula

The Profitable Private Practice Playbook

7 Ways Private Practice Owners Leave Money on the Table Every Day and How to Fix it

Nneka Unachukwu, MD

ENTReMD
PUBLISHING

Copyright @2024 Nneka Unachukwu

All rights reserved

The Profitable Private Practice Playbook

7 Ways Private Practice Owners Are Leave Money on the Table Every Day and How to Fix it

ISBN: Paperback 978-1-963503-03-6

ISBN: Ebook 978-1-963503-04-3

ISBN: Hardcover 978-1-963503-05-0

To the brave unicorn physicians who are still building
private practices in the midst of unprecedented challenges.
You are exactly what healthcare needs!
Thank you for staying in the fight.

Table of Contents

Introduction

love seeing physicians win. This is our time. We're ready to thrive.

That might sound like a crazy thing to say since there's a lot of darkness in the healthcare space right now. But, even though things might seem hopeless, even though a lot of physicians are scared—and rightfully so—I feel hope.

First, let's take a realistic look at what's happening right in front of us and all around us.

Only 30% of private practices are owned by physicians these days, and that number continues to decrease. Not too long ago, that number was 46%. There were 11,000 practices that either went out of business or sold to private equity in 2021. For the first time in history, more private practices are owned by hospitals and private equity than physicians.

That's some really bad news.

A lot of doctors are feeling the financial instability, the burnout, and a loss of autonomy—and shutting down or selling their practices. But I'm here to tell you that I'm surrounded by physicians who have found a way to make their practices profitable. They're thriving right now in these uncertain times.

That can be you too.

I'm a pediatrician by training. I've been in private practice for 14 years. At this stage of my career, my main focus is helping amazing physicians just like you embrace entrepreneurship so you can have the freedom to live life and practice medicine on your terms.

If you're reading this and you're a physician who owns a private practice, you're a fellow unicorn. If you're *not* a physician who owns your own practice, you're still welcome to hang out with us in these pages.

If you're shy or introverted—or don't feel like an entrepreneur—I get it. That was me just a few years ago. I started off as a socially awkward introvert. I never in a million years would have believed I could be an entrepreneur.

But we are physicians. We do hard things every single day. We learned the Krebs cycle; we intubate little babies; we replace hearts.

We can figure out entrepreneurship.

Why I Wrote This Book

As a physician, I love to serve and provide value. I wouldn't have spent all that time and money to become a doctor if I didn't. I talk a lot about a disease I call "learn-itis" that's very common among physicians, where we love to learn, but we're learning to *know* instead of learning to *do*.

This book—and my business school—aren't about learning to *know*; they're about learning to *do* so you can see the results. Will you know more after you read the book? Of course. But the magic happens when you start *applying* what you've learned.

This book came about as a result of a five-day online workshop I hosted in September 2023 for physicians who are private practice owners. We talked about the seven ways we leave money on the table in our practices every day, and it was so powerful.

When I host something like this, I see it as my job to show up like people paid $10,000 to be there. If someone paid 10 grand, I know I would want to deliver a return on investment of at least 10X. So that means you can potentially create at least 100 grand out of what we're about to learn.

The second part of the equation is that the person attending the event (or reading the book) needs to show up like they paid 10 grand for it.

I want you to pretend you paid $10,000 for this book.

You lean in with an open mind, curiosity, and optimism—and a determination to follow through and put what you learn into action. That's what the physicians attending my workshop did, and they're already seeing results.

Even though I knew the event would be a powerful experience, I couldn't have imagined just *how* powerful. It was powerful for everyone who attended, because they got a whole lot of valuable information for free. And it was powerful for me, because it gave me an opportunity to talk about things that I've done—and helped others do—for years now. It helped me to show these physicians what is actually possible with a few simple changes.

For the people who made the decision to join my EntreMD Business School, yes, they're going to go further faster, but the truth of the matter? Anyone who attended the workshop and applies what they learned will get results.

I ended those five days with so much hope for the physician community—and, in particular, for the physicians who run private practices.

Here's How I *Don't* Want You to Read This Book

I see three big mistakes people make when they read a book—or attend a workshop or conference—and I want to spare you from those mistakes.

Mistake #1: approaching it with pessimism. If you open a book with a negative, skeptical mindset, you're not going to get anything from it. If that's your attitude, don't even bother. You might as well save yourself the hours and dollars.

Instead of cynical statements, ask curious questions like: "Wow, what am I going to learn?" Then "wow, what if I tried that?" It's a very simple flip from "this will never work," to "hmm, I wonder how this could be possible."

Mistake #2: looking for shiny objects. I'm really committed to simplicity. I take complex things and make them simple. I don't look for fads; I look for the timeless classic proven things that have always worked and will continue to work. You probably won't hear things from me that you've never heard in your life. The magic is in the simplification of it, so you can consistently execute on it, so you can get the result.

Don't say "I've heard that before." Ask yourself: "But am I *doing* it? And am I doing it *consistently*?" Repetition is the mother of deep, lasting transformations and impressions. But you've ultimately got to act.

Mistake #3: lack of execution. You've heard the things, you understand the concept, you know what to do, you've done the calculations, you know this will work. If you don't have the intent and the follow-through to execute, then you're not going to create the result. It takes intent, motivation, and accountability to follow through with what you decide to do.

Sometimes people say "I struggle with execution." Everybody does. The most disciplined people do. It's just that they've built mindset tricks, people, programs, and systems in place to hold them accountable. There's nothing wrong with you because you struggle with execution. It's called being human.

If you show up to an event optimistic and curious, and you aren't expecting shiny objects, and you actually execute the strategies you've learned, you will always be a person who gets a return on investment for every event you attend. I do not lose money on events. When I go to an event, I show up, and I get massive results because I do these three things.

And when I read a book, I do the exact same thing. I act like I paid $10k instead of $15, and I get a massive return on that investment.

I'm Here to Give You Hope

In a time when we see so much hopelessness, I want to give you hope. *Real* hope, not false hope. Yes, there are so many challenges out there in our industry—especially for those of us who own our own practices—but there are things we actually have control over *right now*. And we can take control over those while we work on those bigger systemic things that will take longer to fix.

We can enjoy life *today* as we work to change our industry. It's possible. And the proof is in the physicians who are already doing it. As we all become examples of what is possible, there's going to be a ripple effect that is going to disrupt the whole space, and that makes me giddy with excitement.

In that spirit, I wanted to take all that incredible content I shared online and put it in a book. I want it to be accessible in as many formats as possible for as many people as possible, and it was worth the extra time, effort, and money required to write and publish it in book form.

I did not write this book to sell anything. Will you find out more about my year long program for physicians - The

EntreMD Business School? Yes. Will I manipulate, guilt-trip or strong arm you into joining? No. It either is for you or it isn't.

I believe so strongly in what I'm doing and how I'm helping people that I want to tell as many people as I possibly can—and I literally only want people to join who absolutely want to. I'm not here to sell anything. I'm here for one reason:

To help you get what you want.

I showed up for five days. I left everything on the table. And I showed up with the intention of helping people get what they want. And what does a private practice doctor want? They want to be able to serve and they want to be able to earn. We'll talk about that in great detail in the chapters to come.

I'm not driven by how many people I can get to sign up for my program. I'm driven by a deep desire to help physicians get what they want.

This book was born from that desire, and I'm so grateful it found its way into your hands. I want to show you what's possible. I want to show you there's hope.

I want to give you what you want.

7 Mindset Shifts You Need to Make

Before we get into nuts and bolts—and go get that money we've been leaving on the table—I do want us to look at some paradigm shifts we need to make. Now, I know physicians. I know how we think. And some of these might make you feel some kind of way, but we're here to embrace all the things.

Stick with me here. Mindset is truly everything.

Mindset Shift #1: I AM A BUSINESS OWNER.

Sometimes, in the private practice world, we don't want to think of ourselves as business owners. "Business is what destroyed medicine," you might be thinking.

No, business is not what destroyed medicine. Business led by people who put *profits before people* destroyed medicine. When physicians who put *people before profits* do business, they do it ethically, and it makes everything better.

This thought process of "I just see patients; I'm not a business person; I'm not an entrepreneur" is part of the reason we're here. Your private practice is a business. You are a business owner.

What is a business? A business is an entity that serves people in a profitable way. That's it. Business is not a cuss word. I *am* a business owner. I serve people. I make an impact in my community, for my team, for my patients, and I do this in a profitable way.

Profit is also not a cuss word. Every time we think, "Oh, that's bad, that's slimy, that's yucky," we don't do the things we need to do to make our businesses thrive. And that's how we got to the place where only 30% of private practices are owned by physicians.

We want to know how to keep our businesses profitable. We want to know how to stay in business. We want to know how to hire, how to build company culture. We want to understand how to do these things. If you don't have profit, you have to shut your doors, the end.

I'm a proud business owner, a proud entrepreneur. Let's own that. That's the first thing. Repeat after me. I AM A BUSINESS OWNER. And it's okay.

Mindset Shift #2: MONEY IS NOT BAD.

Money is mercury paper with dead people's faces on it. That's it. It is not bad. We don't want to talk about money, but we pay our people with money, we pay our bills with money, we pay our taxes with money, etc. Money is paper. It's not bad. It just *is*.

What *is* bad is putting profits ahead of people. But that's not what we're talking about here. We're talking about money, and we're going to get comfortable talking about money. As we go through this book, we're going to discover seven ways we leave money on the table, so we're going to get comfortable talking about money.

For the most part, we doctors don't go into medicine to make money; we go into medicine to *help people.* So our natural bent is to put people before profit. What that means is that, if *anybody* should have money, it's us, because we can be trusted to use it for good. Money in our hands will lead to a lot of impact for people.

Money by itself is just paper. We have the choice to use the paper to do good or use the paper to do bad. You know which one you're going to choose.

Mindset Shift #3: ONE OF THE BEST WAYS I SERVE MY TEAM, MY PATIENTS, AND MY COMMUNITY IS BY BUILDING A PROFITABLE PRACTICE.

When I started my practice 14 years ago, this was my mission statement: "Ivy League Pediatrics provides expert medical care with unparalleled customer service in a profitable way."

I put the word "profitable" right there in the mission statement. I wasn't afraid to use the word. Why? Because if I don't generate a profit, I have to fire my team. If I don't generate a profit, I can't serve my patients.

At the end of the day, it's my responsibility to be a good steward of the practice and make sure it's profitable so my team can keep their jobs and my patients can continue to be served in a way that makes them feel good. So many of them have told me, "Thank you for staying independent. Here I feel like I'm not a number but a person. Thank you for making me feel like I matter, like my kid matters."

If I didn't build a profitable practice, I'd have to shut my doors. Period.

Mindset Shift #4: NUMBER OF PATIENTS SEEN DOES NOT TRANSLATE TO REVENUE or PROFITS.

You can't just look at the list of patients you served and think that means you got a lot of money. Unfortunately, that's not how it works.

"Wow, what a great month," you say to yourself. "We were so busy. We saw a thousand patients."

Great, but what percentage of those patients did you get *paid* for? If you saw 35 patients in one day, but you collected no copays and no deductibles and you were tired, so you didn't send your super bill over to the biller, then guess what. You saw the patients but you didn't get paid.

There are other business activities that need to be done before patients seen translates into revenue. If you don't do those things, it really doesn't matter how many patients you see. Your practice won't be profitable.

Mindset Shift #5: THE SYSTEM IS WHAT IT IS. FOR NOW.

I know the healthcare system is an absolute mess. I'm not saying it's not. It is what it is. Are we coming for the insurance companies? Yes. Are we going to fight for what's right? Absolutely.

But for right now, at this moment, we're going to figure out how to thrive in the midst of the chaos. We're going to put our own oxygen masks on first, or we won't be able to help anyone else.

I know you want to thrive in private practice while we figure out what to do with all these other big systemic issues that won't be solved in a day or a week or a year—or maybe even 10 years. We're going to work on that, and we're going to thrive in the meantime.

In this book, we're going to address those things that are actually inside of our control *right this minute.*

Mindset Shift #6: MY TEAM EXISTS TO HELP ME WITH THE MISSION OF MY PRACTICE.

When you start reading about all the ways you're leaving money on the table in your private practice, I don't want your mind to go to "how in the world can I get all of that done?" I want you to automatically think of your team.

I want you to think about *delegation.* I want you to think to yourself, "I can put this thing on this person's plate and that thing on that person's plate." I want you to spread the love, spread the work.

Your team exists to help you with the mission of your practice. Don't get stuck thinking that "these are not the tasks a front desk person does" etc. Think of your team as an extension of you. You work together to make your mission a reality.

We physicians are known for trying to do it all. We don't do well with delegation. That has to change right now. We're going to delegate delegate delegate.

There's no such thing as a thriving practice without it.

Mindset Shift #7: I CAN'T FIX EVERYTHING.

I know some of you are thinking, "I have 2000 things to fix in my practice. I don't even know where to start."

We're not going to fix all 2000 things in this book, but I'm going to tell you where to *start*. I'm going to show you seven ways you're leaving money on the table every day, and you're going to work on fixing those seven things.

If you think about every single thing you need to fix, you're going to be overwhelmed, and you're going to do nothing.

We're not going to try to fix everything. We're going to identify these seven areas, we're going to focus on them, and we're going to fix them.

Now you've got your mindset right, you're ready to do this, so let's go.

Take our Private Practice Profitability assessment to see how your private practice measures up. We will tell you the most critical changes to make first to improve the financial health of your practice. Go here www.entremd.com/privatepracticebook

EBS Physician Spotlight: Dr. Leslie Golden (Obesity Medicine, Wisconsin)

Why did you join the EntreMD Business School?
Dr. Golden: When I started, I was a partner in a family medicine private practice. At the time, I wasn't intending to launch my own private practice. I just wanted to feel more confident and understand business more as the junior partner in the practice I was in.

How has EBS improved your way of life?
Dr. Golden: I would have never thought a year and a half ago that this is where I'd be. My life is so different. It's so exciting, the impacts that I'm having in my community. It's just incredible. I never would have been able to do any of this without EBS, without the structure, without the support.

What has been your biggest tangible win?
Dr. Golden: Within a year's time, I became known for what I do. My practice became so busy, and I learned so much about business and marketing within this time. By the end of the year, I started thinking, I think I'm just going to do this on my own and decided to launch my own practice. April 3rd, 2023 was my first day at launching my own practice, and I launched it fully booked and within two weeks. I had to hire another provider. In the past few weeks, we started tearing down walls, because we're expanding into the suite next to

us. We are on track to cross our first seven-figures in revenue in our first year.

What has been your biggest intangible win?

Dr. Golden: The mindset that I now have, like everyone says, it's night and day different. I believe in myself, and I believe that I'm my net worth. Dr. Una likes to talk about how you become your net worth and invest in yourself. I was never willing to invest in myself, and now I don't even think twice about it. Of course I'm going to invest in myself. What else would I invest in? I'm definitely going to follow through more than any other investment.

CHAPTER 1

Front Desk Losses

I f you skipped the previous section on the seven mindshifts you need to make before you go get your money, go back and read them. I'll wait.

I'm not kidding, my friend. The nuts and bolts don't work if you don't get into the right mindset first. We're going to shake up our own practices—and private practices around the country—but not until we believe we can do it and take action.

There are a lot of doctors in this country at their wit's end, crying out for help. The hundreds of doctors who showed up to my challenge were people who were saying "I'm not giving up on my patients." That's you too, isn't it?

You could have quit. You could have thrown in the towel and said, "I'm not doing this anymore." But you didn't. You're going to find a way to make this work. You want to be part of the solution to the problems we're facing in healthcare today. If we all rally and come together, we can make such a difference.

The most important thing to know about me is that I love doctors, and I really believe that this is our time. Yes, things are challenging, but we're absolutely 1000% going to get through it. We're going to embrace possibilities from an optimistic viewpoint; we're going to learn some new things; we're going to apply what we learned in our practices; and we're going to see exciting changes.

We're here for solutions. We're brimming with hope. We're full of energy and ready to get things done. And it's going to be amazing.

Simple, Not Easy

I am here to make things simple for you. I want you to embrace things that are simple. You're not going to read about complex, overwhelming solutions in this book. We're going to be talking about things that are simple but profound. Simple but will produce results. Simple but will change things in a massive way in your practice.

I'm not saying it's *easy* (although some of it will be); it's just not *complicated*. You still have to do the work. The good news is that my team and I have worked very hard to figure out the very best ways to help you get that money you've been leaving on the table. We've worked hard on ways to help you increase the profitability of your practice *right now*, not six months from now or two years from now. *Today*.

I'm going to show you example after example of little thing after little thing. But, when you weave it all together, we're talking $100k, $200k, $400k, or more that you can add to your practice over a space of 12 months. It's going to blow your mind.

Will you do me a favor? As you read, will you promise to stay curious? Will you open your mind and ask yourself questions like: *How could I use this? How could I apply this? How could this work?*

Don't tune out on me. Don't dismiss something because it seems too simple, maybe even too easy. Don't make assumptions or think, "Oh, that's not happening in my practice."

Pay attention. Investigate. Be curious. And watch the magic happen.

It's Time to Take a Close Look at Your Front Desk

When it comes to your private practice, the front desk is so critical. In a way, your front desk team and your billing team are the aorta of your practice. If it gets nicked, you bleed out. The number one way private practice owners leave money on the table every day is uncollected money. Uncollected money is a nick in the aorta of your practice.

You might say, "Oh, we don't do that. We collect all our money."

I'm going to stop you right there and ask that you not make assumptions. Once upon a time, I had just changed EHRs, and the reporting capability was so fantastic. I used to go around bragging that, in my practice, you couldn't go past the waiting room if you hadn't paid your co-pay.

"We run a tight ship," I said smugly.

Aaaand the joke was on me. We ran the numbers, and our gross collection ratio was around 80%. I was shocked and horrified. I literally had no idea. So much for that tight ship.

Don't be cocky about this until you actually audit your practice. Go in and investigate. Run all the numbers. Find out exactly what is actually happening, not what you *think* is happening.

Why Isn't the Money Getting Collected?

So what's happening? If you find out that you have uncollected money (and you almost certainly will), why is it not being collected? There are a few reasons.

When it's time to collect your co-pays, do you have patients that smile at you and say "Oh, I didn't bring any money with me today. Can you bill me?" And like the good doctor you are, you say, "Of course."

And you never see that money.

It's the same thing with deductibles and old balances. They already owe you $1000. They come in for another appointment and say, "I didn't get any statements. This is the first time I'm hearing about this balance."

You've got to collect co-pays, deductibles, and old balances. I know you want to be nice. I know you are an empathetic person and have a heart to serve. But you can't serve these patients if your business isn't profitable and you have to shut your doors.

A lot of times, people's membership cards or credit cards on file don't work. Either they expired or they were canceled. So you don't get paid.

Maybe you have poor procedure capture. Maybe you have labs that were done and recorded in the charts, but they didn't make their way over to the biller. Maybe you have procedures that are extra that you didn't charge for. You might have insurance companies that don't cover certain procedures, but you feel bad, so you do the procedure anyway. You do lead testing or an eye test because it's good for the patient, and then you eat the cost.

Does any of this sound familiar? You are seeing yourself here, aren't you? You don't collect co-pays, deductibles, or old balances. Patients have credit cards on file that aren't working. You do procedures that nobody pays for.

And, I repeat, if you're thinking, "This doesn't happen in my practice," go into the office tomorrow, pull up your reports, and take a good, thorough look.

If you haven't specifically trained your front desk people to collect this money *no matter what*, they probably aren't doing it. They're nice people, just like you, and they don't want to ask people for money. That patient just gives a sad smile, and your front desk person says, "Don't worry about it. We'll bill you."

I'm not asking you or anyone on your team to be heartless. You're just collecting money that people owe you. You don't buy groceries at the store, then tell the clerk, "Oh, I'm sorry. I left my wallet home. Can you just send me a bill?

Yes, your private practice serves people. And it's also a business that needs to be profitable to keep its doors open.

People tell me, "I'm doing a lot of pro bono." I hear you, but let me remind you: your practice does not have an endless reservoir of cash. If you don't have more cash coming in than cash going out, it's only a matter of time until your practice has to close its doors.

You're not a charity. We're helping people, but we're not a charity. If we were a charity, we'd raise millions of dollars to cover the costs of helping all those people. We don't have the luxury of generous donors financing our operating costs and payroll.

We're also not the federal government who can just borrow a trillion dollars from who knows where any time they need it. We are our own ecosystem, and we have to stay profitable if we want to continue to serve.

I won't stop saying this, because it needs to be said until you internalize it and act accordingly. After you read this book, I want you to treat this very differently than you have been up to now.

Inefficient Insurance Verification Systems

So, the first way you're leaving money on the table is by not collecting the money you are owed, whether that's copays, deductibles, or old balances.

The second way is an inefficient insurance verification system. This specifically applies to physicians who are insurance-based. Remember the paradigm shift we talked about. You don't get paid because patients walk through the door. There are other things that need to happen in order for you to get paid.

What happens when someone at the front desk checks-in patients with a specific insurance company that you're no longer contracted with? Or what if you administer a procedure that their insurance doesn't cover? Then you have no way to get the money from them, and you're paying for it out of your own pocket.

Think about how quickly one unbillable well check visit per week can add up to hundreds and thousands of dollars you left on the table. I'm inviting you to see this as an opportunity to go back and look, to make sure that what you think is happening is actually happening. Embrace this opportunity to look under the hood.

In the past 60-90 days, have you had a patient who a.) either didn't have insurance or b.) had insurance you're not in network with or c.) had a procedure their insurance didn't cover? How are you going to get that money? You're not. If this is happening in your practice, you have to put a stop to it. And you can't know if it's happening until you start paying attention.

Let's walk through some solutions, so your team can start working to make sure this money isn't getting left on the table day after day after day.

You Have to Help Your Staff See the Connections

One of your most important responsibilities as the CEO of your practice is helping your staff see the connection between their job, their salary, and the bottom line. It might seem obvious to *you*, but it's not to *them*. Most of the time your staff members have no idea where their salaries come from. A common statement in my practice is: *your salary does not come from my 401k.*

You can't expect them to read your mind. You have to actually tell them that their salary comes from the work we do here, the revenue we generate here. Your staff needs to understand that the fact that we saw somebody today doesn't mean we got paid.

You need to tell them: if you're collecting the insurance information and you're not collecting it correctly, there's a chance we won't get paid. And if we do get paid, it can take a long time. But you want to be paid every two weeks. And I want to pay you every two weeks. If there are payments that fail, we need to know. We need to recover them. This is how we get paid. This is how we keep the doors open. This is how we pay the mortgage here.

You're going to say this nicely. If your front desk people want to tell patients, "It's okay, you can pay later," do they want you, their boss, to say that to them? "I'll pay you later. Instead of getting paid every two weeks, just bill me, and I'll get around to it."

You've got to sell them on this idea. Don't expect them to think like the boss. In all fairness, when you were an employee, you probably didn't get it either. Then you became the business owner.

As the business owner, it's your job to help them make those connections. You have to help your team understand that *this* is how this works, *this* is how you continue to get paid, *this* is how we stay profitable, *this* is how we continue to provide amazing service to our patients. *This* is why so many practices shut down and we're still here.

We're the ones who will train and coach them, so they get it, so they make the connection. Most people don't make the connection between what they do and the bottom line. You have to make them see that collecting money is their number one priority—not sending faxes or doing spring cleaning. The money doesn't come in, you don't get paid. Period.

Talk about it. Explain it. Answer their questions. Cast the vision. Don't ever assume they inherently know how things work. They don't. Once they get it, then that's just the way your practice operates. It becomes the culture.

You Have to Train Your Staff On Specifics

We're not just talking about pep talks and making mental connections here. You have to actually train them on the specifics to ensure that the practice gets paid. You have to show them how to collect the insurance information. You have to explain what is primary and what is secondary insurance.

You have to enforce your rule that we don't let people go past the door if they didn't pay their co-pay. Explain that we used to bill people for co-pays because of course they'll pay their bills. Until they didn't.

Train them how to respond to people who say they can't pay their copay. Train them to tell a patient: "Your copay is $35. How will you be paying for that—cash or card?"

Let's say the patient says, "Oh, I didn't know. I didn't bring any money for that." You train your front desk staff to smile and say, "Okay, well, there's an ATM down the street, or we're happy to reschedule the appointment." They have to be okay with this response. Tell them, if it's hard at first, it gets easier. If it never gets easier, maybe this isn't the job for them.

As far as the patients go, when my front desk people say this to them, well, you wouldn't believe the miracles that happen. They'll sigh and reach into their pocket, and that cash or credit card just magically appears. It's wild.

Sometimes we think, "I shouldn't have to train my people. They should know what to do." It doesn't work that way. If you want to have the best team, you'll train them. The end.

"But if I train them and they leave, then it was a waste." No, you became good at training. The worst thing that can happen is that you don't train them and they stay.

Remind the front desk and the billing team that they're the aorta of your practice. It might sound dramatic, but it's not. If your front desk is bleeding money, your practice—and their jobs—are not long for this world.

Hold Them Accountable Until It Becomes the Culture

So number one, you help your staff see the connection between their job, their salary, and the bottom line. Number two, you train them on the specifics to ensure that the practice gets paid. And number three, you hold them accountable until that becomes a new pattern, until it becomes the culture.

If you tell your front desk that we're collecting co-pays and all of that, you need to make sure you're measuring it, that you're keeping a close eye on it. You can't just say it; you have to follow up.

Ideally, you're not the one doing this. If you have an office manager, it can be part of their job. They can ask questions at the end of the day and run an audit:

- What percentage of the copays today were collected?

- What percentage of the deductibles were collected?

- Who came in today with an old balance and we let them go?

- Who came in and their membership expired four months ago and we still let them in?

- Did we let someone come in whose insurance we're not in network with?

- Did we do a procedure for someone that wasn't covered by their insurance?

You're looking at those on a daily basis until it becomes a habit. You can train all you want, but if the accountability isn't there, the behavior doesn't change. You have to go all in, stay on top of it, and make it clear that this is how your practice is going to be run, no exceptions.

A profitable business doesn't leave money on the table, and you need all hands on deck to make sure that all of that money goes back into the practice so they can get paid.

In the next chapter, I'm going to walk you through some team losses. But first, I'd like to introduce you to a very special friend of mine.

Dr. Ebony: A Case Study

Sometimes all of this can be hard to visualize. It's helpful to see an actual physician who is doing these things in her actual practice.

I'd like you to meet Dr. Ebony. She's a solo pediatrician in Atlanta, GA, who realized she was leaving a lot of money on the table in her practice every single day, and decided to do something about it. She started running her numbers and found out some incredible things. And she's going to share those with you.

Oh, one thing about Dr. Ebony: I made her up. But here's what you need to know: everything in this scenario is absolutely realistic and possible. Let's go through it together, and you can tell me if doing this work is worth the effort.

Dr. Ebony sees 25 patients a day. Of those 25 patients, 15 are sick visits. She ran the numbers and realized they had 4 missed $35 copays a day = $140/day. They also had 2 missed old balances of $100 each per day = $200/day.

That's $340/day x 260 working days = $88,400/year

This is $88,400 left on the table for work that was *already done.* How many of you would be okay recouping $88,400? How many of you are like whoa, wait a minute, I can't afford to lose $88k a year?

There's more. Dr. Ebony found out she had a front desk person who was letting people with a specific insurance company come in that she was no longer contracted with.

One unbillable well check visit per week = $300/week and $15,600/year.

Between her uncollected monies and her inefficient insurance verification system, Dr. Ebony was losing $104,000/year. That's six figures. Left on the table. And the saddest part of this is that this is *profit*. She already paid the staff, the mortgage, the utilities, the front desk person who's failing to collect this money, all of that. This would have been *profit*, straight to the bottom line.

We're already at six figures and this is only strategies #1 and #2. She's got five other ways she's leaving money on the table. Fortunately, Dr. Ebony read this book, and she fixed it. She recouped $104k that went straight to the bottom line.

Let's Be Like Dr. Ebony

We've got to be diligent. Seeing the patient is not what translates to revenue. Seeing the patient *and getting paid* is what translates to revenue. We are good physicians who love people. It's so tempting to tell ourselves, "It's no big deal. I'll just do this thing. It's okay if I don't get paid."

It's not okay. You need to run a profitable practice if you want to stay in business and keep serving these wonderful patients as your wonderful physician self.

You can't worry about all the money you've left on the table in the past. That's over and done with. Going forward, you're going to make changes. Don't assume you're fine. You're going to audit, and you're going to fix it.

Don't believe the lie. No, private practice is not dead. We can say "insurance reimbursements have decreased." We can say "the great resignation made it so hard to hire." Those are true. The system sucks, and we'll work on the system. But first, we need to take care of what we can control. It's 100% within your power to fix, and I'm rooting for you. You can be just like Dr. Ebony. Yes, she's a unicorn, but so are you.

It's time for our practice revolution. This is our time, and we're going to do it right. We're going to win and we're going to thrive, and we're going to be examples of what is possible so other people can thrive in their private practice too. It's time for the pendulum to swing the other way, so that 70% of private practices can be owned by physicians, instead of 30%.

We haven't even left the front desk, and we're already at six figures. We've got five more ways to go. Next up, we're going to talk about losses that come from the rest of your team. How can you get your team on board so you're not alone, trying to work out the profitability of your business?

I'll show you.

Take our Private Practice Profitability assessment to see how your private practice measures up. We will tell you the most critical changes to make first to improve the financial health of your practice. Go here www.entremd.com/privatepracticebook

EBS Physician Spotlight: Dr. Ed Wing (OB/GYN, Virginia)

Why did you join the EntreMD Business School?

Dr. Wing: I kept listening. I kept paying attention, listening to all the content Dr. Una put out there. And I thought, you know what, I think I just need to make a decision to join and to make this work, to find the time to join, to find the money. I said to myself, look, if all the things she's saying are true, then I'll be able to make back my money by just doing the things she says.

What has been your biggest win since joining EBS?

Dr. Wing: It has been quite the journey, and it's pretty amazing the difference six months in EBS has made. One of the things we did is set up our quarterly goal-setting system, and one of my goals was to reach a certain revenue. Prior to EBS, I had tried to hit it for literally years and was just not able to do it. And after the first quarter, I hit it for the first time, and it wound up being the biggest revenue intake I'd ever had in my private practice of 10 years.

What can physicians expect from EBS?

Dr. Wing: You know, EBS really has been a support both through the community and the things I've learned from Dr. Una and others, and I expect to just have great things, even through all this craziness in the healthcare space.

CHAPTER 2

Team Losses

So we've looked at front desk losses, which are so important, because the front desk touches the money so much. Next up is team losses, but before we get into that, I want to talk a little bit about why it's important for us to be profitable.

My practice doesn't have an endless budget and neither does yours. We have to figure this money thing out—and we can. We physicians do hard things every single day. This is no different.

Why a Profitable Practice?

How many of you truly want to put yourself in a position where you can live life and you can practice medicine on your terms? I know that's what I want, and I bet you want that too.

Listen, I love what I do. I want to take care of my patients, but I want to do it in a way that is consistent with me practicing the way I believe I should practice and having a life I love. We worked so hard to get here to not have a life. I want to live my life and love my life.

The truth of the matter is this: to practice medicine on your terms, you require financial freedom. To *live life* on your terms, you require financial freedom. At the end of the day, everybody is going to exit their practice one way or the other, because you're not going to live forever. You either have a kid who will take over the business, or you sell it to another physician/corporate entity, or you shut it down.

At the end of the day, we're all going to exit.

What do we need if we're going to exit on our own terms? We need a profitable, well-oiled entity that can work without us. This is your ticket to practice medicine on your terms, live life on your terms, and exit on your terms.

When you think of it this way, you'll want to just get down to business and do this. It's possible. I'll give you examples to prove it.

Yes, things have been tough lately. Yes, people feel stuck. Yes, insurance companies are a mess. But I want to give you examples of what real physicians are doing, so you can get inspiration from it. Instead of throwing your hands up and saying you can't do it, I want you to ask:

What if it's possible for me?

We've had doctors in our EntreMD Business School who built their practices and reached the 7-figure mark in a year. We have someone who crossed that mark in 15 months. We've got doctors taking a family vacation every quarter, and they're in the same crazy healthcare space that everyone else is in. Some people want 10 locations. Some want to retire early and enjoy their family. Whatever it is they want, they're going after it, and they're on their way to getting it.

These things work. Maybe somebody has told you they don't. They do. This can be your reality. You can choose your own schedule. If you love to work, you can work five days a week. Or four, or three, or two. You get to choose.

Think about it. This is not just about numbers. This is about intentionally creating the life you want to live. We are big believers in building your dream business and your dream life at the same time. But you cannot do that without profit.

I want us to make a decision here. I want you to say: I *choose* to build a profitable private practice. This is all about changing the way we think. It's very different from the narrative out there, but you're reading this book with a bunch of unicorns, and we are doing unicorn-y things.

I choose to build a profitable private practice. This is my responsibility. Why? I want to practice medicine on my terms. I want to live my life on my terms. I want to exit on my terms.

I choose.
I choose.
I choose.

Now that we are all on the same page, let's talk about team losses. This one is going to knock your socks off.

Poor Coding Habits

When we talk about the team losses, we're going to start with one that nobody wants to talk about. It's something you might be doing, something your team might be doing. And it's costing you money every single day.

Poor coding habits.

I know, I know, we shouldn't have to talk about this. This should not be so complicated. But remember, the system is what it is for now. We can't fix it overnight, and we're not waiting for the insurance companies to get their act together before we go after our dream life. So we're not going to argue about this. This is one of those times when we learn the rules of the game so we can win at the game (whether we like it or not).

When I started out in private practice 14 years ago, I didn't know anything about coding. I probably would've broken out in hives if you tried to tell me about coding. So I did what every responsible physician would do, which is bill all my E&M visits as 99213s. I really didn't want to get audited. I didn't know the rules. I had heard that, if you billed sick visits as a 99214, you'd get audited. So I just did the safest thing. I coded everything as a 99213.

Then I discovered that this, just like everything else, is a skill. "You can learn this stuff," I told myself. And so I learned it. And it added thousands of dollars to my bottom line every month. It was the craziest thing. I was seeing the same patients, delivering the same care, but I had been undercoding.

Side note: maybe you're thinking "I'm DPC, so it doesn't matter." It actually does. Hear me out on this. Yes, the insurance-based practices undercode and get smaller payments from the insurance company. But the DPC physicians essentially undercode themselves by charging a whole lot less than they should, for no other reason than the mind drama around raising prices.

So I figured that out; I fixed it for myself; I was seeing more money come in; and I thought, "Okay, we're good." Then I hired other doctors to work with me, and guess what happened. They were doing the same thing I'd been doing. The poor coding was no longer a problem for me, but these other physicians were still coding 97% of everything 99213. I wasn't undercoding, but *they* were.

Maybe you're not undercoding, but your team might be. Do you even know what their percentages are? You have to look at it for yourself, then for your team. They may not know what you know. If you made these mistakes in the past (especially the recent past), then there's a good chance they're making them too.

You can't make assumptions. You have to check.

The data shows that, the longer you stay in private practice, the worse your coding gets. Isn't that wild? You start penalizing yourself for your competence. You've got to stay on top of it. What's your percentage of 99213s? 99214s? 99215s?

You've got to know what's happening in your practice and not just assume.

Now, let's talk about the money we're leaving on the table each time we undercode.

No two insurance companies are the same, but the average difference between a 99213 and a 99214 is about $35/visit. The average difference between a 99213 and a 99215 is about $60/visit.

Think of it like this. When you see a patient who is a 99214, and you bill them as a 99213, it's like handing that patient a $35 gift card out of your bottom line. You might as well be saying, "I'm the doctor whose bank account is a bottomless pit of money that never runs out! You get a stimulus check! And you get a stimulus check! Everybody gets a stimulus check!"

But you're not Uncle Sam. You're not a charity or a nonprofit. You don't build a profitable practice by handing out gift cards every visit.

Go take a look at your records. For yourself and for your team. Please don't make the assumption that you're not undercoding. We're not here to make assumptions; we're here to do audits. Go look. If anyone on your team is doing this, you're paying their overhead and supporting their gift card-giving habit. I highly recommend you stop.

The solution here is really to learn to code. Practice it. Audit it for yourself and your team until it's a habit. Train your team. Show them how it's done. Monitor their percentages.

Do chart audits. Anything that has to do with money in your practice, that's your aorta, your bloodstream. It's dangerous if you don't know how to do this (or your team doesn't).

You might say, "I don't want to talk to my team about this." Let me ask you something: do you want to thrive or not? If you watched the physician working with you sign company checks or hand out gift cards paid for by you at every visit, you would stop them. That gets really expensive really fast.

So you're going to learn to code; you're going to practice this until it's second nature; you're going to train your team to do the same; and you're going to audit audit audit.

Got it? Great. Now, this next one is really fun.

The Unfilled Schedule

As you know, I'm a pediatrician. Back in the day, come summertime, pediatrics was dead. Kids aren't in school. Parents go on vacation. Everything gets super slow. So I was brand new in practice and I would see some of the older docs say, "It was really dead today. I had to send two of my team members home."

Think about that for a minute. If you send your team members home, you're either paying them for work they're not doing, or more likely, you're not paying them. And they still have bills to pay. They still have a mortgage. Your team is important to you, and you want to take care of them. This isn't how you do it.

I had just switched my EHRs and started using PCC (Physician's Computer Company), and one of the things I really love about it is the reporting capability. Then I discovered a way of pulling up a report of every patient in my practice who was overdue for a check up, and I smiled. "We are never going to have a slow summer again," I decided right then and there. "That is never going to happen."

So what did we do? We called people and told them, "Let's get you an appointment for this summer. You definitely want to miss when everyone's going back to school. You don't want to be here then. Everybody and their mom, their relatives, their cats, and their ancestors are all going back to school—and they'll all be in the doctor's office at once. Let's get you in right now when it's nice and smooth and less crowded."

We had whole pockets in the schedule, and we knew they weren't going to get filled with sick visits, so we leveraged that "sales pitch" and did a bunch of check-ups all summer long.

I had told the team, "It's either this, or I have to send you home." We took a team approach, got everyone on board, and had our most productive summer ever.

You don't just accept whatever the schedule brings. For a pediatrician, the summer brings nothing. You create your schedule proactively. You're not just passively waiting. You play offense, and you build the schedule you want. We don't wait around. We create it, engineer it, make it happen.

I have so many people tell me, "Things are really slow right now. I don't know what to do about it." I'll tell you what to do about it. You make that choice, and then you do what you need to do to fill that schedule.

Let me ask you this. How many of you, when the schedule is light, see your team breathe a sigh of relief and say, "Oh, this is such a good day, such an easy day, there's hardly anyone on the schedule…."

Have you ever seen your team celebrating something that was almost making you cry? They're celebrating no patients on the schedule? This isn't cause for celebration. How do they think everyone gets paid? This all goes back to making sure your team understands the connection between their job, their salary, and the bottom line.

If they want to keep their job, if they want to keep getting paid, then we need to be a profitable practice. And that can only happen if we're filling the pockets in our schedule.

When you look at your schedule, and there are empty pockets, I want you to look at it as an open wound that is actively bleeding. Only instead of bleeding blood, it's bleeding dollars. As a physician, you know you need to suture this and stop the bleeding. You need to fill these spots.

When we start thinking this way, we develop the creativity to fill it up. And we're training our team to do the same. You want to help your team see things through your lens. That's why you need to meet with them, cast the vision, and get them on board. Your team can't read your mind. They won't know these things unless you tell them.

Now, listen, maybe you're thinking, "Dr. Una, sometimes we have a killer day or a killer week, and I'm fine with a slow day every now and again. We need it to help us recover."

If you're fine with a slow day, because you almost died yesterday, that's up to you. You can make an executive decision there. I'm not talking about running your team into the ground and not caring if they burn out. Of course we don't want anyone to burn out from exhaustion. I'm talking about consistent holes in the schedule that could be filled if you just get creative.

Maybe you're thinking, "I don't have this problem. We're full enough." Let me just remind you how quickly things can change. This was something I knew before the pandemic, but the pandemic just drove the point home.

Things can change so quickly. You can be fine one minute and not fine the next. You want to be agile enough that, if something happens to your schedule, you know what to do. You know what levers to pull, what to ramp up, how to ramp it up, etc. So you can respond to anything and everything that comes your way. Even something as "unlikely" as a pandemic on a global scale.

What are you going to do if CVS sets up a MinuteClinic next door? What if the hospital sets up a practice a block away? What if a major referral source decides they're no longer sending people to you? It doesn't take much.

You have to understand that business is mountains and valleys. So when you're on the mountaintop, you want to be thinking: if there's a valley-type situation coming up, how do I prepare for it? How will I respond?

Let's talk about some ways to get that schedule filled, so you're ready no matter what comes your way.

Practical Ways to Fill Your Schedule

First of all, let's see how much money we're leaving on the table with each empty slot in our schedule. I'm going to use $200 as the average revenue per visit. If you don't have anybody scheduled at 9:30, 12:00, or 3:30, that's $600 you're leaving on the table.

People who know me know how optimistic I am. So this is not about getting down and depressed and sad and worried. It's about knowing how to interpret what is happening properly. It's about maximizing your profit in your practice every day.

So how are we going to fill this schedule?

First of all, you want to define your target daily average volume. What do you want that number to be? And factor in your no-show rate, your last-minute cancellations. If you want to see 25, schedule 28-30 to cover the last-minute no-shows. If everybody shows, you'll figure it out. Just get creative.

The second thing you're going to do is watch it like a hawk. Look at your number yesterday and today and tomorrow and next week and two weeks from now, so you can anticipate. If you notice that, 30 days out, you usually have twice as many patients on the schedule as you have right now, you can respond ahead of time instead of when it's already too late.

The third thing is your internal marketing. If you think about it, there are tons of people in your practice who need appointments, whether it's someone with hypertension that you need to see every three months or a two-month-old who needs to come for her four-month check-up.

You aren't marketing to new people here. You're bringing your own people back in—patients who are overdue for a visit and just need that reminder, that nudge.

We did a lot of internal marketing during the pandemic, and we were busier during the pandemic years than we were in the years before it happened. Sometimes, when it's slow, people want to send faxes and do spring cleaning. No. If you have a slow day, call the people who need appointments. Work your internal marketing.

Internal marketing is all about leveraging the patients you already have, and it's so much easier and cheaper—and effective—than external marketing. But, don't get me wrong, external marketing is very important too.

External marketing is the fourth thing you can do to fill your schedule. External marketing is limitless. You can build referral sources, speak locally, engage in social media groups where your target audience is and you're known as the expert there. There are so many things you can do. You're really only limited by the amount of time and money you want to spend doing it.

The bottom line is that we have to play offense, not sit around and wait and see what happens. We can create the schedule we want. We have to be agile enough to make the schedule look the way we want it to look. We're the bosses here. We make things happen. It's up to us.

Are You Fine With Leaving $300k on the Table?

Are you ready to hang out with Dr. Ebony again? We're going to run some numbers for her, and I'll warn you: they're going to be a little crazy. I want you to look at them with an open mind.

Dr. Ebony has four 99214s billed as 99213s per day. Remember, there's a $35 difference. 4 x $35 = $140/day. And $140 x 260 (working days in a year) = $36,400.

She also has five unfilled spots in her schedule per day. She has the bandwidth for 25 but has only scheduled 20. 5 x $200 = $1000/day / $1000 x 260 (working days in a year) = $260,000

Total: $36,400 + $260,000 = $296,400.

Once we see this, we can't unsee it, and we act accordingly. Dr. Ebony left $296,400 on the table by undercoding and having an unfilled schedule. That's it.

We've only explored two of the seven ways we'll discuss in this book, and they total almost $300,000. Add the front desk losses, and that's another $104,000. We're already over $400k.

I'm just going to let that sit for a minute.

What could you do with an extra $400k? That might pay off your student loans. You might finally be able to get that next critical hire. You might be able to upgrade your office space. That might be more than your annual salary.

Pull up these numbers and look. Look for yourself and your team. What are you waiting for? I know what some of you are waiting for. I've heard the excuses.

"I don't want to look at coding. I don't want to talk to my team about this. I'm not comfortable talking to referral sources. I don't like doing social media. I'm not good at it."

If you're going to make $400k extra, *get good.* It's that simple. Get good at it. I don't know, man. For an extra $400k in pure profit with no additional overhead?

Maybe do it.

I want you to think about this. Think about Dr. Ebony—this nice, lovely pediatrician who provides great service and is adored by her patients—who handed out $400k in gift cards last year. Then she attended my workshop (or read my book) and gave herself a $400k raise. So far. With more to come.

You have two choices. You can hear this and be inspired and go start running audits for yourself and for your team. You can even say, "I can't conceptualize $400k, but I can conceptualize $200k."

Or you can be cynical. "That doesn't really work. Social media doesn't work where I am. I can't ask for referrals. My insurance companies don't pay $200 per patient."

I want to invite you to please not do that. We are here creating history. We are here setting ourselves up to be examples to the physician community that you really can build thriving practices in this day and age.

I want you to take the bet on yourself. I want you to take the bet on principles that are proven. I want you to take the bet on that and say, wait a minute, I can do this. That's the commitment I want from you.

I want you to say: "I am going to do this. I am going to go look at what I'm doing and what I need to change. I am going to do the work."

I want you to look at yourself in the mirror and say, with confidence, "This cute face is going on social media. I'm going to go to all the potential referral sources in the area and tell them to send me patients. I'm going to do all the things. I'm going to do my internal marketing, call all my patients overdue for appointments, and train my team not to throw a party when the schedule is empty."

You think asking for referrals is uncomfortable. Of course it's uncomfortable if you aren't doing it regularly and getting more comfortable with it. How do you start asking for referrals? You're going to walk up to somebody; you're going to have a big smile; you're going to introduce yourself; you're going to tell them what you do; then you're going to ask them questions about themselves.

Then you ask them the million-dollar question. "As a pediatrician (for example) in the area, how can I support what you do and give your moms a great experience with their kids?" You ask them. Let me tell you what. Many people aren't asking them. But you're not most people. You're going to actually do it.

Asking becomes comfortable *when you ask*—and not a moment before. Ask ask ask ask ask, and at some point it clicks, becomes comfortable, and it's just what you do.

Until you get comfortable, I think a little discomfort is worth $400,000 extra. What do you think?

The next chapter is all about owner losses, the ones you have the most control over.. That can be both scary and empowering. Let's go get that money.

Take our Private Practice Profitability assessment to see how your private practice measures up. We will tell you the most critical changes to make first to improve the financial health of your practice. Go here
www.entremd.com/privatepracticebook

EBS Physician Spotlight: Dr. Brittany Panico (Rheumatology, Arizona)

Why did you join the EntreMD Business School?

Dr. Panico: My friend, who's a dermatologist, was sort of urging me, "When you're ready, start a practice, because we need more people out here. I'm doing it, and I think you could do it." So he put the bug in my ear, but of course I was thinking, I don't know a thing about business. I've been employed my entire career. So I came across the Visibility Formula workshop hosted by Dr. Una, and I thought, oh my gosh, this is my ticket to learning all of the things that I need to learn to be able to open up my own practice.

What has been your biggest win since joining EBS?

Dr. Panico: I think the mindset is such a key portion of it because we learn what it means to provide that investment back into our community and how we can pivot our role and our service to accommodate for that. So one of the things that has happened in just the last couple weeks is that a private practice closed. So there has been a change and shift in the patient population, and a lot of those patients needed to be seen quickly or were without infusion medications and we sort of capitalized on that by increasing our social media and increasing our word of mouth in the community about our work here and opening an infusion center. If you're somebody on infusions, we're here for you. I think it's about taking something you're already good at, getting better at it, and being more vocal about, "I am the person who can do this for you in this community." It's just been really great because of the return: the patient volume, the filling of your schedule quickly. Being full after only six months has been my return. I'm not struggling to see patients, and that's such a big relief, and putting in the work that Dr. Una talks about in EBS, the success that other people have had and the tools they're using, and saying, okay, I can apply this to my specialty and my practice.

What can physicians expect from EBS?

Dr. Panico: The investment is just the seed. It's just the tip of the iceberg that starts this big snowball of all these other things. And a lot of it isn't until months or maybe even a year later. But once it starts to come, it starts happening faster and bigger each time, so that's been really rewarding.

What difference does a year with EBS make?

Dr. Panico: It's so incredible to think that all I had to do was make that decision, and now it's automatic. I came up for renewal, and it's like, yes, not even a question. I had already budgeted to renew. It's really that decision that this is what's gotten me this far in a year, so if I do it again, it's unfathomable what can happen.

CHAPTER 3

Owner Losses

This chapter is going to be super powerful, because it's all about you, the boss. This is your zone. You may be able to delegate some of this, but when push comes to shove, it's your hands. You're the boss. I need you to own this.

Say it with me: *I'm the boss of my practice.*

I'm the boss. This is my identity. I'm going to take charge and create changes in my practice. I know how to create revenue. I know how to create a demand for patients. I understand how to maximize profits. I understand how to lead a team.

I'm the boss. I'm the boss. I'm the boss.

The two losses we're going to talk about in this chapter might not seem very exciting at first glance, but when you see how damaging it can be if you *don't* take care of them, you'll be excited. I guarantee it.

An Unmonitored Revenue Cycle

What if I told you that you never had to meet with your biller ever again? Would you be okay with it, maybe even really happy about it? You're not alone.

I get it. It's not fun. It causes anxiety. When I first started out in private practice, I didn't know anything. I'd look at the spreadsheet and break out in hives in my mind. I was like, "I don't want anything to do with this."

But when it comes to the way that money comes into and leaves your practice, I want you to go back to that aorta imagery. When you nick it, you bleed out. We've got to stop the bleeding. Yes, the bleeding is money, and yes, we've got to stop it.

As the boss, you want to build a practice that's sustainable and profitable, so you can continue to take care of your patients, so your team can continue to have jobs, and so you can create financial freedom for yourself and your family.

And, someday, you're going to want to exit that profitable practice of yours, and you want to exit it on your terms.

Because we want all of these things, we're going to do whatever it takes to make them happen.

Part of what it takes is monitoring your revenue cycle, monitoring what is going on in the billing department. Some of you might be thinking, "I'm direct primary care, and that doesn't apply to me." If that's you, I want you to extrapolate here. In your case, you want to make sure all your memberships are current for your patients. Is that something you're staying on top of? If your answer is "I don't know," then you're not. I guarantee it.

Let's come back to the insurance-based practice. How does this look? It looks like avoiding a meeting with your biller. You don't want to have conversations with them. You may be thinking that, as long as there is money in the bank account to pay the bills, payroll, and the mortgage, I don't want to know what's going on. The only time you'd talk to the biller is if it looks like there's not enough money to take care of the business.

If you find yourself in that position of avoiding your biller, you are leaving tons of money on the table.

If this seems overwhelming and daunting, I want you to remind yourself that we are physicians. We survived medical school. We can figure this out. We deliver premature babies that weigh less than a pound. We can figure this out. We do knee replacement surgery. We can figure this out.

You can survive a meeting with a biller. I promise you.

If you find yourself thinking this way, remind yourself that you're the boss of your practice. You show up. You do what needs to be done.

I'm the boss. I'm the boss. I'm the boss.

Maybe you do meet regularly with your biller, but you're not really looking at anything, because there are no metrics.

Have you ever had a meeting with the biller, and they're like, "Everything's good!" and because you don't want to mess up a "good thing," you say, "Great!" and that's that?

Sorry to burst your bubble, but a "great" meeting with your biller where you didn't see any metrics is not a great meeting with your biller.

You want to have metrics. You want to know what your A/R (Accounts Receivable) should look like in the different buckets (< 30 days; 31-60 days; 60-90 days; etc.). What does that look like? Is it going up? Down? What do the denials look like? Where are write-offs being done?

There are certain metrics you need to know, so that you can have the meeting with your biller and make sure the money's working.

Remember, you do not get paid because you saw patients. You get paid because you saw patients *and* you did other things to make sure you were paid. Sometimes the number of patients on your schedule is very deceptive because, if you're seeing them and not getting paid for them, you might as well not have seen them.

The unmonitored revenue cycle is a big deal. We're not doing that anymore. We're not avoiding biller meetings. We're going to monitor our revenue. Some of you reading this actually did oral boards, and you came out fine. You can do a biller meeting.

Where are these losses happening? Sometimes they're with denials. And there are tons of reasons why there may be denials. When you look at the data, some would say as many as 35% to 50% of claims get denied the first time. But there's a ton of money left on the table because 60% of denials are never reworked. People just shrug their shoulders and move on. Nobody goes back to say, why was this denied, and what can we do to get it approved? The data also shows that it costs anywhere from $30 - $177 to rework a single denied claim.

Where else do we have losses? Let's say your biller sends out the claim and says, "We charge $260 for this," and the insurance company pays you $260. Any time the insurance company pays you exactly what you asked for, you undercharged. If they paid you exactly what you asked for, then chances are, on your fee schedule, that number is higher. If you undercharge, they're like, "Sure! You only want $75? Here you go! We'll give you that!

So, whenever the number is the same, you should wonder why.

Another thing to note: the things that get inspected are the things that get done. Are your claims being filed on time? You know you don't get unlimited time to file, right? Let's say you have 180 days to file a claim, but no one checks to see if it was filed, and somehow it doesn't get filed. Now it's too late. The window has closed, there's nothing you can do about it, and you eat the cost.

The problem is that sometimes these are small amounts ($50 here, $100 there), and you think, "Oh, well. It doesn't matter." Hold tight. Dr. Ebony and I are going to show you that it *does* matter. So here's my question for you:

Are you going to start meeting with your biller?

Remember, you don't get paid because you saw a patient. You get paid because you saw a patient, the coding was done properly and the billing was done properly (and on time).

So meet with your biller. And when they tell you everything is okay, don't believe them. It's not because they're liars. It's because the things that get inspected are the things that get done.

All right. What's the second owner loss?

Staff As an Expense vs. Staff As an Investment

Whenever someone tells me, "I can't afford to hire staff," I know they're looking at their staff as an *expense* instead of an *investment*. Staff as an expense means they *cost* you money. Staff as an investment means they *make* you money. This is a huge difference, and your mindset around this can make or break your business.

In this section, we're going to talk a lot about revenue-generating activities. I want you to ask yourself: "In my private practice, what are the activities that generate revenue?" And I want you to get very clear on this.

Let me back up a minute and explain this. Some of you might be thinking, "Dr. Una, you don't understand. I don't care about all of this. I just care about taking care of my patients, and all you're talking about is the money. Money is what destroyed health care."

Money did not destroy health care, okay? What destroyed health care is people putting *profits before people*. But, for health care to work, you need the people *and* the profits. For your practice to work, you need to serve *and* earn.

Now, if this was a clinical book, we'd be talking all about the serving. But here we're talking about how to work the earning so we can *continue* serving. When we talk about building your practice so it's profitable, we're talking about keeping the earning going so you can keep the serving going.

Once the earning stops, the serving stops.

I want you to take a deep breath before you keep reading. Breathe in. Breathe out. Relax. Lean into this. There's nothing bad happening here. You haven't sold out because we're talking about money. You are doing what you do as the boss of your practice to continue to earn so you can continue to serve.

You are a physician. I don't need to ask you if you put people before profits, because that's how we're built. I know that's who you are to your core.

So, with that in mind, let's get back to revenue-generating activities.

What Exactly Are Revenue-Generating Activities?

Once upon a time, back in the day, I'd say, "Oh, we have a slower day, great. What do you guys want to do with the day?" And my staff would say things like, "Oh, we have all these faxes to catch up on, and we want to do some spring cleaning, and we want to take care of some paperwork, there are some things we need to shred...." And I'm like, "What are you talking about?"

None of those things I mentioned just now create any revenue. If my staff spent a day doing all of those activities, I would still have to pay them for the day. I'd have to pay them with revenue that was not generated. In other words, I'd be paying them out of my own pocket.

So I started training them on what revenue-generating activities are—and how it relates to their paycheck. Now, I'm not saying your staff can never do a single thing that doesn't generate revenue; it's just not the number one priority.

I ask them: "What's a revenue-generating thing you can do today—and also do these other things—so we can get what we want?"

Maybe one person says they have a whole list of people with outstanding balances. They can call and collect those. That's a revenue-generating activity.

Somebody else says they can pull this recaller and call everyone who's a year and under and due for an appointment. That's a revenue-generating activity.

Someone can do this, someone can do that. Even if it's a slower day with less patients, your staff can still create revenue, so your equation (revenue = paycheck) still works.

You want to start thinking about which tasks, out of the hundreds they could do, will actually move the needle financially. Which ones directly generate revenue? Once you're clear on that, you can empower your team to join you in this mission to build a practice that serves *and* earns.

When you have a team, and there is no thought of RGAs (revenue-generating activities), it just puts them in a position where they don't know why they're there or what they're doing. Let me give you some examples.

For a medical assistant, one of the metrics could be, "You're already working the patient up. Before they leave, make sure you've scheduled their next appointment, so no one leaves without a next appointment." What that means is that, if you see 20 patients a day, you might have 15-20 future appointments scheduled that day. That could be 100 appointments a week. If you have a medical assistant who has created 100 appointments, they are revenue-generators. This is something they do that affects the bottom line.

Let's say you have a scheduler and their job is to make sure that, for each of the five doctors working in your practice, they have 20 appointments on the books each day. The scheduler's job is not to schedule when people call. The scheduler's job is to make sure the schedule is *full*. Do you see how that's different? There are so many different ways to fill a schedule. How they do it is up to them, but their job is to do it. And, remember, we already looked at the consequences of an unfilled schedule.

Your front desk person has a simple metric. For everyone who checks in, make sure we have a 100% collection ratio for our copays and old balances. When your front desk person does this, they're a revenue generator.

With your office manager, you want to start thinking about not just tasks, but outcomes. In this practice, these are our monthly goals, these are our yearly goals. So you're not just delegating *tasks*, you're delegating *outcomes*—and the thinking and creativity that goes into making those outcomes happen. If your admin team does the admin tasks in such a way that the people generating revenue have more time to generate that revenue, then the admin is also a revenue generator.

I'm going to add one more that might seem obvious: your doctors. "They're already seeing patients," you say. "That's generating revenue." Yes, it is, but there's something else they can do. They can leverage their voice and reputation to make it more likely patients will come back for a follow-up or well check. All it takes is a simple: "Everything looks good. We're going to see you back in three months, and my nurse Amy will set that up for you." The patient trusts the doctor more than the rest of the team most times, so they're more likely to follow through with that appointment.

You need to be thinking in these terms: my team is an extension of me; we're all working together for one mission. We are here to generate revenue. That's how people get paid. My staff is not an expense; they're an investment. Most of the time, the owner of the business is the only one thinking about things on this level. When you unleash your team to think about—and understand—revenue-generating activities with you, now we're in business.

Are You Sanctioning Incompetence?

The other way we throw away money is when we have what we call "sanctioned incompetence." You have a team member who's not pulling their weight, not getting the job done, destroying your culture because of their attitude. You're not just throwing money away with these people; you're also running the risk of your A players quitting, because the culture is toxic.

Too often, we don't want to confront that person and de-hire them. So we hire other people to do their job, and we let them stay. You can't run a profitable practice this way. If this staff member isn't generating revenue, then they're an expense, not an investment. And it's especially detrimental if they have a bad attitude on top of their poor work ethic. With these kinds of people, you only have one choice: you de-hire them. In our practice, we use the word "de-hire" instead of fire. If you hire someone, and it doesn't work out, you just de-hire them.

Bottom line: it's too expensive to keep the wrong people on your team.

Speaking of expensive, do you have a physician doing work in your office that someone else on your staff could do? Do you have a doctor handling portal messages instead of a nurse? Do you have doctors returning calls for labs when someone else could make those calls? Are they prepping charts or giving vaccines when someone else could do that? If there is anything a doctor is doing that someone else in the office could do, it's expensive. Why is the $350/hour person doing tasks that a $20/hour admin could do? That's costing you so much money.

The same goes for you, the boss. When you're in the office, you shouldn't be doing any task that someone on your team could do. That's expensive. Tell yourself: I'm going to practice at the top of my license. I'm going to do what only I can do. And I'm going to delegate, delegate, delegate the rest.

Now, let's see what these owner losses look like in Dr. Ebony's practice.

Checking In with Dr. Ebony

Let's take a look at our dear friend, Dr. Ebony.

Exactly 10% of her claims were denied and 30% of those were not reworked (15 claims) = $3000/month.

The cost of reworking 35 claims/month at $30/claim = $1050/month.

She also had 4 unpayable claims due to untimely filing = $800/month

Total hours lost per day doing tasks that can be delegated = 1

Total number of patients who could have been seen in that time = 3

Total revenue lost from unseen patients = $600/day = $12,000/month

Total monthly losses = $3000 + $1050 + $800 + $12,000 = $16,850

Total yearly losses = $202,200

If you add this to the $400,400 from the first four strategies, we're at $602,600 right now.

Dr. Ebony is leaving $600k on the table every single year.

What Are Your Options?

Are you feeling overwhelmed? Don't be. Yes, you need to tweak some things. No, you probably can't tweak all of it at once, but for every single thing you change, you're giving yourself a raise. For every single thing you change, you're making your practice more stable. Even if you only recover *half* as much money as Dr. Ebony did, that's still $300k you didn't have before.

Yes, times are different. Yes, there's a Great Resignation. Yes, insurance companies are doing what they're doing. But, YES, we can create raises for ourselves. We can. 1000%. If Dr. Ebony can do it, so can we. Once you see it, you can't unsee it. If you think this is wild, wait until the next chapter.

Take our Private Practice Profitability assessment to see how your private practice measures up. We will tell you the most critical changes to make first to improve the financial health of your practice. Go here
www.entremd.com/privatepracticebook

EBS Physician Spotlight: Dr. Cheruba Prabakar (OB/GYN, California)

Why did you join the EntreMD Business School?

Dr. Prabakar: I was like, wow, this is what I need. This is the group that I need to be in to give this a shot. If I'm going to open a private practice with aaaallll these people around me saying you can't do it and all this negativity, I was like, let me just see.

How has EBS improved your way of life?

Dr. Prabakar: It's really been about more than just the business. It's been a life experience. That's how I would describe my journey with EBS and Dr. Una. It's not just about the business education. This is not just about the nuts and bolts of how you start a business. It's all the things—the mindset, the discipline, stretching yourself in ways you didn't know were possible. I'm in year three of EBS and that's one of the reasons I stay. I don't even know what I don't know. I know more this month than I did last month, and I knew more last month than I did the month before. I feel like I'm moving in these concentric circles, and there's no end really. I'm going to be in this school for life, I think.

What has been your biggest tangible win?

Dr. Prabakar: Within 14 months of being in EBS, not only had I overcome that fear of starting a practice, I actually left my job, opened my own Direct Specialty Practice (GYN), and had patients scheduled. And this was all with three kids, by the way.

What has been your biggest intangible win?

Dr. Prabakar: It's prevented me from burning out, honestly. There was nothing inherently wrong with my job before, but I knew there was more. But I did not have the people to get me to that more. You know, sometimes they say there are no shortcuts in life, right? But there are, and EBS is one. It's a big shortcut to getting to where you want to be, because people have figured it out, and they're leading the path before you. With people burning out all around me, I don't feel that way, because I'm just so energized every day. Going to work is fun for me.

CHAPTER 4

Thriving in Private Practice

I am constantly paying attention to my physician community and what they need. In this chapter, we're going to take a little bit of a detour. I want to paint a picture for you before we get to the rest of the strategies. (And let me just tell you that #7 is so wild.)

It's really important to me that you can see the possibilities no matter where you're starting from.

A few years ago, I'd be in Facebook groups where, almost on a daily basis, people were so frustrated, saying they were ready to shut down their practice, throw it all away. Day after day I'd see this, and it got to the point where I thought, "We've got to do something about this. We're in it now. We have to do something."

I have to do something. I want to help physicians thrive in private practice. I know I can help. I know it doesn't have to be this way.

We don't have to feel stuck. We don't have to be at a loss with no idea where to turn. We don't have to say things like

"I'm just a lowly broke pediatrician" or "I'm the bottom of the food chain as primary care."

We're not going to be content to whine in Facebook groups about the dismal state of affairs in private practice. We're not going to do that. We're going to gain control, find solutions, and make things happen.

There is a better way. And once you see it, you can't unsee it.

Let's Take a Look Behind the Scenes

So I've been in private practice for 14 years at this point, but let's start at the beginning. Right out of residency, I started working for a doctor who owned his practice but didn't work in it. Technically, I was a solo pediatrician. I'd show up like a boss, see the patients, do the thing.

But here's the thing. On the very first day I saw patients in my own practice, I walked out of the room after the first visit and felt... nothing. It was anticlimactic. I had worked so hard for so long and spent so much money, and this was it? I'm going to do what I just did 20 times a day until I'm 70? I couldn't imagine it.

I still can't.

So I made a decision right then and there that I was going to do this until I turned 40, and then I'd retire. I've got nine lives, I told myself, and I'm going to live every single one of them.

Now, is this a prescription for everyone? Of course not. I'm not even recommending it. I'm just telling you what I wanted, what I decided. In the world of business, you get to do whatever feels right for *you*. Maybe you want to practice medicine for 50+ years. It's up to you.

My dad was a surgeon. He was reading anatomy textbooks until the day he died at 84. He was doing surgery until he couldn't any more. It was a calling. His calling, not mine.

I was a socially awkward, introverted introvert, so entrepreneurship was not a thing that was on my radar. Not at all.

When my one-year contract was almost up, my boss said, "We need to talk about your contract." He gave me a five-year contract. I had just finished my three-year residency and I had been married for three years, so three years was an eternity to me. And *five* years? I couldn't even fathom that. I told him I couldn't do it because I was going to move.

"If you're going to move," he said, "you should start your own practice."

I thought he'd lost his mind. Nobody starts their own practice 15 months out of residency. This was 2009. Nobody was doing that. Well, no one I knew did anything like that.

"The things you're doing here," he told me, "you're already solo. I can help you if you need it, but you should start your own practice."

Did I mention I was pregnant with my second child?

That didn't faze him. "Your practice will be a baby," he said, "your baby will be a baby, and by the time your practice is so busy that it needs more of you, your baby will be grown."

This was a classic case of ignorance is bliss. I didn't know the full extent of what goes into running a private practice, so I said sure! And I started researching. I pulled up websites, looked at other private practices (Facebook groups didn't exist back then), found a place to lease, signed it, and started talking to insurance companies.

I was under the impression that I would hang the shingle and they would come. "You're a good physician," I told myself. "Just hang the shingle, and things will just start happening."

Boy, was I in for a rude shock. I hung the shingle, me and my good pediatrician self. And guess what. They did not come.

That's when it dawned on me that I was going to have to go *tell people* about my practice. Now, remember, I was a socially awkward, super-shy, introverted introvert. You mean I actually have to *talk to people*? And ask them to *send me patients*? Isn't that slimy and yucky and manipulative? I'd be no better than a sleazy used car salesman. Ew.

So I didn't do it. And guess what—the patients didn't come.

I was like a deer caught in headlights. "What have I done to myself?" I thought, in a complete panic. But I had signed a lease. I couldn't just walk away. If I could have, I would have. That's how terrified I was.

By this time, I had a two-year-old and a four-month-old, and I was running a practice literally all by myself. I was my own medical assistant. I was my own front desk staff. I was my own biller. Someone would call the office, and I had a front desk alter ego. Her name was Ella.

"Thank you for calling Ivy League Pediatrics," I'd say when I answered the phone. "This is Ella. How can I help you?"

I once had someone call and say, "The doctor's name is kind of strange. Does she have a thick accent?"

"Oh, I don't think so," I told them. "You'll understand everything she's saying."

This is hilarious to me now, but it wasn't funny at the time. I had such a scarcity mentality that I couldn't imagine paying someone to join my team. My team consisted of exactly one person—me. I took the calls, saw the patients, administered the shots, made the next appointment, and sent the claims to the insurance company. That's how wild it was.

I finally gathered up enough courage to go to the nearest OB-GYN, because what better place for a pediatrician to find patients, right? But I was scared spitless. I didn't even have the nerve to ask for the office manager, let alone the physician. I just talked to the person at the front desk.

Then one day, I was reading a book by Brian Tracy called *Eat That Frog*, and I had an epiphany.

I Decided to Build a Thriving Practice

"All business skills are learnable."

I read those words of Brian Tracy's, and it jolted me out of my scarcity mindset for the very first time. I had always looked at other practices around me and thought, "Oh, I'm nothing like them. They know everything, and I don't."

Reading the words "All business skills are learnable" blew my mind. I suddenly realized that, when you see people doing things at a much higher level than you, they're not *better* than you. They just have a skill you don't have yet. But you can learn it. I can learn it. Because all business skills are learnable.

That book was such a turning point for me in my life and career that I've probably recommended it to at least a thousand people.

I'm a physician. If there's anything I know how to do, it's *learn*. Doctors are learners. We can acquire skills. We did it in medical school and residency and we keep doing it. We're constantly learning so we can serve our patients better.

So I started looking at private practice very differently. What skill do I need to acquire to thrive here? I started learning. I got mentorship. Then the practice started working.

Ultimately, I learned all these business skills and I said, "Okay, I'm going to build a practice that thrives." I didn't care what anyone else was saying or doing. I didn't care what was happening in any other practice. I was going to build a practice that thrives. I was going to build a practice where I could practice how I wanted to. I was going to build a practice where I could create financial freedom for myself.

I decided that was what I was going to do, and I got to work. Within two years, I hired someone to work every Friday, so I could have a long weekend every weekend, because that's what I wanted. I have at least five other practices within a five-minute drive of me, but we were still thriving.

To retire at 40, I needed to build not just a practice, but a business that could run without me and I do it. At 40, I started seeing patients once a week. My definition of retirement is seeing patients because I want to as opposed to because I have to. I couldn't let go of my stethoscope though. When you've been doing this for decades, it's kind of just part of you. As I write this, I've been on a "sabbatical" for two and half years and the practice is still going. It generates over a million dollars in revenue every year, is profitable and has a great team that leads it. I succeeded in building an asset that thrives without me.

I also knew I wanted to homeschool my two older kids (I have four), who are 16, and 14 years old. They were A students and that was great. But the more I thought about it, the more concerned I got. If they get As in school until they're 18, and then they go to college, has this prepared them for life? Like real actual life?

You might wonder why I was thinking this way. I'll tell you why. I went to school for a long time, and I wasn't prepared for *anything* that really mattered. I didn't learn personal finance. I didn't learn business. I didn't learn leadership. And I was terrified of speaking in front of people.

I've taken one for the team, and I've decided it will be different for my kids. I'm going to let them do school online, then I'm going to teach them business, leadership, money management, real estate, entrepreneurship, and maybe most importantly—confidence.

So that's my dream—and that's what I'm doing. I've been homeschooling them for the past three years because that's what I want to do. I love mentoring people. Oh my goodness, I just love helping people become the best version of themselves. I'm able to do that in so many different ways—including with my own kids.

And it's all because I made the decision that I would build a thriving practice—and I took the action I needed to take to make it happen. And now I want to help other physicians do the same.

I Want Freedom for My Fellow Physicians As Well

When I see what's happening in the physician community, and I see what I've been able to achieve and build in my own practice and life, I know I can be part of the solution.

Building the practice I built, in the way I built it, gave me the freedom to go all in with the EntreMD. And what do we do at EntreMD? We help doctors build profitable 6-, 7-, and multiple 7-figure businesses, so they can live life and practice medicine on their terms, whatever that is. It's not about what everyone else is doing. What do *you* want?

You pay the price to build your practice, make it profitable, and build a business system around it that gives you the freedom to do whatever you want.

There really are no excuses.

So you're an introvert. So am I. I'm still an introvert and a very private person. I've just learned to overcome that when I need to.

Maybe you're a pediatrician. So am I. In the grand scheme of things, we're not the highest paid physicians. Everyone knows this. On top of that, I see a lot of Medicaid patients in my practice.

Maybe you don't have a business degree. Neither do I. You don't need one.

Maybe you have small children. When I started this, I was a mom of little kids. They're still all school-age. If you have little kids, this is still in the realm of possibility for you.

"But what about the problems that come with being an entrepreneur?" you say. What about it? It is in the face of problems you find out whether what you're doing works or not. When the pandemic hit, it was pure chaos and confusion all around us. I started looking around, asking, "Okay, what is our response to this?" Nobody knew what was happening or what it was all going to mean, but I came out with guns blazing and wasn't about to accept defeat.

We pulled together some traditional business skills, and built a strategy that worked. In 2020-2021, we did better than we did in 2019. Then we brought in more revenue in 2021 than in 2020. All because I made the decision right then and there: I'm going to thrive in the midst of this. Period.

And I did.

We can whine and complain, "Oh, the reimbursements are so bad. Private equity is doing this, the hospitals are doing that." You might say, "I'm tired. I just want to sell it. I want more time."

First of all, a profitable private practice will sell so much better than one that's not. And second, the more profitable your practice, the more time you'll have for yourself.

But it all starts with a decision. *I'm going to thrive.* I'm going to figure it out. I'm going to do what needs to be done. I'm going to thrive.

Don't believe the lie. You can build a thriving practice. You can. And I'm inviting you to choose to do so. This is a choice. And you can decide to thrive. You can decide I'm going to acquire business skills. I'm going to learn how to attract clients, how to create revenue, how to build a team, how to do this and live life on my terms.

What is your dream life? Write it all out. Get it all in front of you. The sky's the limit. What do you really truly want?

That's what's going to drive you to do the work.

What If You Could Actually Have a Weekly Date Night?

Now, just so you don't think I'm the only unicorn out there—and that you can't possibly be one yourself—I want to share some more stories with you than just mine. Dr. Ebony's story is powerful, but yes, we made her up.

I want to introduce you to some real-life physicians who will show you what's possible by sharing their own personal stories. We're going to start with Dr. Ngozi Ude-Oshiyoye.

Dr. Ngozi is a fellow unicorn. Her specialty is family medicine, and she co-owns a primary care practice with her husband who is also a physician. They have been open since 2016.

Dr. Ngozi joined the EntreMD Business School a year and a half ago, but she had been listening to my podcast and watching my videos for six months before that. A lot of huge changes have happened for her over the past two years, "and it's been amazing," she says.

When I interviewed her about her experience, she was just chill and smiling, like she didn't have a care in the world. "Has entrepreneurship always come easy to you?" I wanted to know.

She says that's "laughable." No, it hasn't. She has three children, and her kids were young in 2016. Her youngest is now six. Right before the pandemic hit, she had no medical assistant. She had "one-and-a-half" front desk staff. At one point, she and her husband were both working seven days a week. They had every other weekend off, but they never took off the same weekend because of child care. They literally did their date nights *at the hospital cafeteria.*

I don't know about you, but that doesn't sound like a dream life to me.

But things are night and day different now. So I asked her to paint a picture for us and help us see what her life looks like now. What does her team look like? Her family life? Her date nights? How is her practice doing financially? How many hours and days is she spending at work? I want us to be able to envision that picture.

Dr. Ngozi told me that their practice now has two physicians (she and her husband) and three nurse practitioners. They're open seven days a week 9-5. Her husband works at the hospital every other week, and she recently went down to four days a week.

They have an amazing team, which includes an in-person staff for the front office as well as a virtual assistant who works to support the practice. They now have an office administrator, which was a big step for her. She had tried to hire an admin in 2018 but never followed through. In hindsight, she says, "it was just mind drama." The impostor syndrome came on strong. What would she tell an admin? Who was going to want to follow her? The relief at being able to get an admin who knows what they're doing is indescribable—such a huge burden lifted.

In addition to assembling that A team, their revenue is so much higher this year than last year which was a seven-figure year. They're not only profitable; they're scaling up. It's so much better than it was before.

"It's hard work," she says. "It's not perfect." There's still a hiring problem everywhere, and they're working through that. She says the biggest thing for her has been shifting her mindset. "When you fix the inside, everything around you changes."

Her next goal is to get down to three days a week. On the homefront, she's looking for an assistant to help her with her home and kids. She's had a lot of applications but hasn't found a good fit yet. But she already has so much more time with her children. She and her husband have date night every single week—they never miss—and it's not in a hospital! She's also added a spa day to her calendar every six weeks.

"Every facet of my life is better," she says.

Which one of us wouldn't like to be able to say that every facet of our lives is better? Not perfect, not challenge-free, but everything's working, and it's so much better.

I asked Dr. Ngozi what she would tell people who are considering joining the EntreMD Business School.

"I think you should do it," she said, without hesitation. "And it's not just the coaching that you get. You get suggestions and examples. The community is huge. Being in community, you get to see what other people are doing, you get to ask questions—even questions you didn't realize you had. And I think that's the big one. You're in a private group where people are posting. We get to bounce off ideas, get answers to your questions.

For me, the books of the month are huge. You're not going to get every single thing. You still have to implement and break away and do your own thing. It's just all of it together. Just do it. When I joined, I had probably listened to the EntreMD podcast for six months to a year. I knew I had pushed myself as far as I could go on my own. I needed to do something different if I wanted to scale. So I would really encourage anyone who's thinking about it to just do it. You're definitely not going to regret it."

Again, this is not for everybody. But if you want to be competent at attracting clients and creating revenue—and building a dream life *while* you do it—then this is for you.

Let Me Introduce You to Another Unicorn

Dr. Tolulope Olabintan (Dr. Tolu) is the CEO and co-founder of a family medical center in Texas. The center's tagline is: "We help our patients live long and well because we believe the quality of life is just as important as the quantity of life."

Dr. Tolu says she couldn't always deliver that sentence with the efficiency, eloquence, and confidence she does now. She joined EntreMD in November 2020. She finally accepted that it was time to open a practice, because she knew it was something she was called to do. For perspective, people who went to medical school with her are shocked that she started her own practice. Business just wasn't her thing—or so she thought—and then she joined EBS.

When Dr. Tolu introduces herself, it's so smooth—not in the sense of being a smooth talker, but just her confident expression of who she is. It's a beautiful thing to witness. She seems like a natural speaker, so I asked her if that was the case. Did she always have the confidence she has now?

No, she said, absolutely not. She had always expected that patients would just come to her naturally "because I'm a good doctor." She didn't know she would have to actually get in front of people and ask for their business.

She remembers one of the first assignments I gave after she joined EBS—do a Facebook Live. She thought I was nuts. That's not something doctors do. But then she had mindset shift after mindset shift. Number one was asking for what she needed. Number two was asking people to come work with her, because what she has to offer is good. She learned that she didn't want to be the world's best-kept secret. People won't just come to your office. They have to know about you to get to meet you.

She'll never forget the first call we had where we talked about sitting in the knowledge of the value of what you offer. I asked them to ask people around them to tell them their strengths, what they're good at. "I was very nervous about that," she says. "I wasn't even sure about the value of what I was offering."

But I walked them through that process, and it was really mind blowing for Dr. Tolu. She learned that what she has to offer is a *gift*, and it's a disservice to not introduce people to that. If you focus on your weaknesses and what you don't have, you're depriving people of a good doctor.

She laughs, thinking back to the first video she did on social media. "I'm glad it's there," she says, "because it shows growth; it shows transformation. It shows what's real." She was holding the phone shaking and giggling when she saw her high school mates join the live. "I introduced myself to the world… and that was the beginning of many firsts, and the success story started from that point."

I love how she says that what she has to offer is a gift, and it's a disservice to not introduce people to that. What if every physician in private practice would think of what they have to offer as a gift? How much easier would it be to put yourself out there, reach out to referral sources, tell people to send me your friends?

What I have is a gift, and it's a disservice not to share.

So where is Dr. Tolu now? What does her business look like? What does her life look like? What is possible when you make the decision that you're going to rise above every challenge?

She is seeing so much growth.Now they're at over 5,000 patients. She crossed her first seven-figures in revenue in her first year. She has a nurse practitioner and just hired a second one. She just put out an ad for a doctor. She has a team of 13 people. There have been challenges, of course— especially with the Great Resignation—but she has become comfortable with delegating and letting other people come up with solutions.

"As long as the outcomes resonate with what I expect," she says, "we're good."

The challenges have been great teachers. Through them, she has learned how to be patient. She has learned how to be a higher version of herself. Challenges no longer freak her out. She calmly asks questions like: *Who do I need to talk to? What do I need to ask? What am I not doing well?*

She has a team that advocates for her and helps put her out in front of more people. Because of the EntreMD Business School, she's actually handling more of the things she wants to do. She's doing a lot with ministry and at home and as a mentor. She has a lot of medical students, pre-med students, even high school students, so she gets to do a lot of teaching, which she absolutely loves.

"I'm not working harder," she told me. "I'm working through good people who are working with me." That's one of the biggest things she's learned through EntreMD. When she started out, she was doing everything on her own. She even had a medical assistant who didn't show up on the first day of opening.

She encourages people to listen well. "Dr. Una is going to teach a lot of things, and everything will change when you do them." Yes, there will be challenges, but you're going to work through them and learn from them.

Dr. Tolu is a firm believer that everyone needs mentors and coaches for every aspect of their lives. Wouldn't it be nice, she says, to have someone championing you and telling you that every goal embedded in you is possible to achieve? She has a health coach for her patients, so in between visits, they have someone encouraging them with those lifestyle changes. She says: wouldn't it have been nice to have that in all areas of my life?

She has that in the EntreMD Business School. "You should watch my videos," she laughs. "You should see the difference. Who I've become through this process is worth every investment to me." And this isn't something she learned from me. She says she was lucky to have that realization right before she met me. Before that, she didn't pay for anything. She was all about watching all the free versions of everything.

"I'm always eager to share my story," she says, "because who I've become is mind-blowing for me." Everyone else is blown away too. Her capacity has increased. They've already outgrown their space and bought the land behind their office. And this is primary care. She's not a plastic surgeon.

We can thrive. We can do this. We're going to need to learn new skills. We're going to need to learn to work through people. Like Dr. Tolu said, "I'm not working harder. I'm working through people." Please see the possibility, embrace the possibility and make the decision—I am going to thrive.

Do You Want to Be a Unicorn?

Do you want to be able to attract the number of patients you want? Do you want to be in a position where you can hire and lead an A-team? Do you want to be in a position where you can create revenue, not think it's a cuss word, and be comfortable talking about it?

I don't know about you, but I want to build something and not die in the process. I don't want to be burned out. I want to learn to do things *through people*. I want to practice medicine and live life *on my terms*. I want to be in community with people who are doing it, get mentorship from people who are doing it. I want to be held accountable.

Unsubscribe from the lie, friends. Decide you're no longer stuck. Decide that this is no longer hopeless. I don't want to hear you say, "Wellll, mine is a little different because…" I want to invite you to open your mind to how this can work for you too.

Imagine if each person reading this book implemented these strategies in their private practice. Imagine the ripple effect in the physician community. The physician community is waiting for people just like you to show them what is possible.

There is no cavalry coming to save us. We're it. We're the ones who are going to bring the change. I want you to understand that history is being written and we have the choice to be the people who will bring the change.

I'm not going to roll over and play dead. I'm going to show up like a boss. I'm going to fill that schedule. I'm going to collect all my co-pays. I'm going to put a picture of my dream life in front of me, and I'm going to create the life I want. I may not be able to do it in 30 days, but I'm going to figure this out.

This is going to happen.

Are you ready to learn about strategy #7? By the time we get done with strategy #7, you will have fallen deeply in love with your private practice. You will decide to do the work, because the results of that will be so wild.

Take our Private Practice Profitability assessment to see how your private practice measures up. We will tell you the most critical changes to make first to improve the financial health of your practice. Go here www.entremd.com/privatepracticebook

EBS Physician Spotlight: Dr. Prem Tripathi
(Plastic Surgery, California)

How has the EntreMD Business School positioned you for success in private practice?

Dr. Tripathi: I think there was more, and I just needed a kick to do it and that's what EBS did for me, create that mindset around the action part. Not learning stuff just to learn it but learning stuff to put it into action. I was thinking about it, but EBS sort of gave me the accountability to do it.

What's a game-changing mindset shift you've had through EBS?

Dr. Tripathi: It's the entrepreneurial mindset, the idea that we as physicians can create successful and profitable businesses, but also that idea that we are not limited to just the skills we have as physicians and at every step along the way, we have questioned our ability and questioned whether the next step was going to be successful. So that part of the mindset has really changed how I step into any situation.

Describe the impact the EBS community has had on your business.

Dr. Tripathi: Every week there's a success group. You designate time to accomplish a task that you've set out to do that week. Being able to create a specific time that you now have set aside so you're able to accomplish those tasks and now you don't have to think about them. That has dramatically changed the way I do things. You can set aside administrative time. We're always scared to do that, because we think it's going to take away from our profit, but in reality, it's going to exponentially improve our impact and our profit.

What has been your biggest win since joining EBS?

Dr. Tripathi: I've implemented weekly sales meetings, revenue-generating activities for our practice. I've tried to make all the roles in the practice more profitable. So those have astronomically changed our impact on our patients, the profit in our practice, the mindset for the entire group of people that work in my office, and even in the time where aesthetics has ups and downs, we've been able to mitigate those downs because we have a set strategy that we didn't have before.

CHAPTER 5

Hidden Losses

told you this chapter was going to be wild, and I mean it. Buckle up, friends.

First, let's recap all that we've learned so far. We've been looking at ways private practice owners leave money on the table every single day. The first six are:

1. uncollected monies

2. inefficient insurance verification

3. unfilled schedule

4. poor coding habits

5. unmonitored revenue cycle

6. seeing your staff as an expense

Before I share Big Number Seven, let me offer this disclaimer: I am not an accountant, a tax strategist, or a financial advisor. This is for educational purposes and should not be considered financial advice. Talk to your tax attorney or whoever is working with you, but I want you to be aware of some very exciting options.

The seventh way that physicians in private practice are leaving money on the table is (drumroll please)...

ignoring second and third generation revenue.

Second generation revenue is passive income earned on the profits of an operating company. We're going to start off this chapter with Dr. Ebony, because I want you to follow along with her as she goes on a mission to create second generation revenue.

This is how I invite you to start thinking: the revenue— the profits—you create in your practice is raw material that you then can use to do other things. Isn't that wild? Maybe you're already doing this. That's great. But I want you to take it further, bigger, higher.

Now, the good news for you is that, with all the strategies you've learned for building a profitable private practice, you won't ever need to shut it down because of cash flow issues. You've got the money coming in, no problem.

At the same time, if something did happen to your practice, and it no longer existed, it can continue to be profitable and make money for you every year, even though it doesn't exist. Or you can sell the practice, and it continues to work. You build the practice to 7-, or multiple 7-figures, and that revenue can go on to create another 7 figures.

This is a very expansive way of thinking, especially if you do it intentionally. So let's go along with Dr. Ebony on her mission.

Dr. Ebony's Mission to Create Second Generation Revenue

Dr. Ebony has just recouped $600k that she had previously just been leaving on the table, and she knows she has to do something with it.

To start, she puts $52k in her 401k. Some of you do this, some of you don't. Some of you do it smaller, some do it bigger..

Next up: she pays her 13-year-old and 10-year-old each $12k/year for a total of $24k, something she just found out she could do. That is now second generation revenue.

Then she heard about something called the Augusta Rule where she can rent her house to her business for 14 days per year and not report it as income and owe no taxes on it. She can use her house once a month for content creation or a high-level meeting. That's another $15k/year.

Her practice is profitable, and she's cash-flowing, so she decides to buy an office building. It has three suites. She uses one for her practice, rents out the other two, and ends up with an extra $24k/year.

None of this has anything to do with her private practice directly. She used revenue that she generated with her practice, but this is second generation revenue.

Dr. Ebony's total second generation revenue: $115k.

How do you like that? I really like that. This is an extra six figures that has nothing to do with her private practice. But she created it after attending one of my workshops. Dr. Ebony was going to stop here, but I convinced her to do one more thing.

Let's Take It One Step Further

All that second generation revenue is wonderful, but it's only the tip of the iceberg. Now Dr. Ebony is going on a mission to create *third* generation revenue. Let me show you what that means.

The money that she paid her kids ($24k) goes into a growth fund. She doesn't just hand the money to her young kids and tell them to have a nice summer. She pays her kids on paper, but the money goes into a growth fund.

What is a growth fund? It's money you put away with which you can invest in real estate, stocks and/or business acquisitions. You can do whatever you want. She has created a growth fund that she uses to fund all of these things. The profit from your private practice is raw material you use to take care of yourself financially. We are doctors. We know how to do really hard things. We can learn how to do this too.

The cash flow from the building ($24k) also goes into a growth fund. The money from the Augusta fund ($15k) goes into a growth fund. The 401k money is already growing on its own.

Now, let's say that, for whatever reason, her practice no longer exists. Guess what *does* exist. The money in the 401k, the money in the growth fund, the cash from people renting out the building. All of her money is growing. Even if the practice is no longer there. This is her insurance policy.

Dr. Ebony's total third generation revenue: Impossible to tell!

In this day and age, so many people are living in fear: what if something happens and I can no longer work? What if something happens and I lose my practice? Let's say something does happen. You're going to be just fine. You have created a revenue-generating engine that is working separate from your practice. You're good.

I highly recommend you start doing this *yesterday*.

Your practice could be working hard for you and creating multiple streams of income. When people tell you that private practice is dead and we're stuck and all of that? Not true. You can make your practice profitable *and* you can create a revenue-generating engine that is separate from your practice.

The discipline is in putting all of this money away—into a growth fund. Imagine that Dr. Ebony put away $24k for five years (her kids are now 18 and 15). That's $120k. Her teenagers already have a down payment for an impressive investment property.

Your practice becomes this thing that keeps giving and giving and giving and giving.

The first six strategies put her in a position to be profitable. The seventh strategy is to then take that profit and keep going, keep it growing, keep investing, keep exponentially growing your money.

When you look at the third generation revenue, it's impossible to put a number on it. There's no limit to this. We can't tell what the number is. We just know it's really good.

Take our Private Practice Profitability assessment to see how your private practice measures up. We will tell you the most critical changes to make first to improve the financial health of your practice. Go here
www.entremd.com/privatepracticebook

EBS Physician Spotlight: Dr. Rachel Rubin (Urology, Maryland)

How has EBS positioned you for success in private practice?

Dr. Rubin: I opened my practice a year and a half ago and didn't take out a loan. I'm a cash pay practice, and I was profitable from day one. And I'm learning to make the math math, and I'm learning to value my own worth. I charge like a lawyer. You want my expertise, you're going to pay for it, and I'm not going to apologize for that, although it took a lot of coaching from this group to get me there.

What's a game-changing mindset shift you've had through EBS?

Dr. Rubin: You all have done hard things. I have done hard things. When you enter the right room, and you realize and celebrate the hard things, and you say, wait a minute, I do it scared always. I was scared when I started medical school. I was scared when I started residency. I was scared seeing that first patient. How hard could QuickBooks be? It can't be that hard. Anyway, I have a million wins.

Describe the impact the EBS community has had on your business.

Dr. Rubin: This is where we're at. All because of the framework and sticking to it, believing in myself and having a community of amazing people helping guide me. "Hey, what do I do with my space? How do I do this? How do I solve these problems?" Everyone's there because they're all at different levels. There are so many incredible students that are so much more successful and farther along than me, and that's the magic of it. I see the future because of them.

What has been your biggest win since joining EBS?

Dr. Rubin: When I opened up my cash pay private practice, I had a waiting list of 350 people. If you call my office, my next new patient appointment slot is in February. I've got problems, people. They're good problems, but they're problems.

CHAPTER 6

We Can Create an Alternate Reality

N ow this is what I want you to do. Pretty please with 17 cherries on top. You have read every word of this book up to this point. This is why I wrote it. This is why I do what I do. Because only 30% of private practices are owned by physicians. And every single day I hear stories of people feeling discouraged, feeling stuck, losing money, like they can't do this any more.

And I just want to say, come on, we can do this. I've done it for myself. These are things that the doctors in EntreMD Business School are doing. We can create an alternate reality. I hope you've seen this throughout the pages of this book. There is hope for us, and we can do this. It is possible.

As you read this, you might feel validated. You're already doing these things and seeing results. I am so happy for you. And what I want to charge you with is: go and spread the word about it. Because so many physicians don't know. Keep doing it, keep crushing it and thank you for being an example of what is possible for physicians everywhere.

On the other hand, maybe, you've heard all of this before, you've thought about it, you're thinking, it makes sense, it really does. I believe I can do this. You know about it, but you haven't done it.

I want to invite you in this pivotal, defining moment to join a community of physicians who are doing this, so you can start this process TODAY. You can learn to attract all the patients you want. You can learn to hire and build and effectively lead an A team. You can learn to work efficiently. You can learn to generate revenue. And you can put yourself in a position where you build a profitable practice, then you start earning second generation revenue, then you start building third generation revenue.

It does not matter what your specialty is. It does not matter where your practice is located. It doesn't matter. There is a pathway for you to win. If that is you, if you know you need the mentorship, the community, the accountability, I want to invite you: **please do not put this book down without filling out an application for the EntreMD Business School**.

Again, there's no pressure, because we only want people who are a good fit and are ready to work hard to build a profitable practice. But do not finish this book without saying absolutely or absolutely not. This is not a joke. Practices are going further into debt every single day. Practices are going out of business every single day. Practices are failing to maximize their potential every single day. There's a way out. This school exists for you. That's why it's here.

You might say you don't have the time, but you *do* have the time, because this business is serious. You'll *make* the time. You might say I don't know if this is the *right* time. Honestly, the right time was a year ago or more, so now is the next-best time. You may say I don't have the money. Business is expensive. Listen, you're either going to give it to Uncle Sam or you're going to invest in yourself and your business.

I don't ask people to do something I'm not already doing myself. My investment in myself (coaching and mentorship, etc.) is a minimum of six figures a year. I'm trying to get somewhere. I'm trying to get something done.

To help make it even more concrete for you, I'd love to introduce you to some doctors who are in the EntreMD Business School and let them tell you about their experience.

This Doctor Watched Her Practice Explode—In the Very Best Way

Dr. Bolanle Akinronbi works in a group psychiatry practice serving people in New York and New Jersey, helping them get well using wellness practices and fewer medications. She joined EBS at the end of 2022 after following me online for a few years. What made her finally decide to join was that she had just begun to expand into a group practice from solo practice and was facing some challenges. She had been listening, learning, and trying to do things on her own and felt like she "needed something more solid and compact, with community support," to really push her to see what else she could do and how far she could go.

She says that "wanting to do more" sounds very cliché, but that's the headspace she was in at the end of last year. She leaned in a little more and asked a few more questions. She didn't feel completely ready, but she overcame her inner struggles and, instead of hesitating like she'd done for years, she decided to go all in.

What was the catalyst? What made her finally say yes? For one thing, she was coming up on a milestone birthday, and it just felt like the right time. She was finally in the right mindset of taking a risk to just see where it went. She also had a few friends who had joined EBS, and she says she had watched them go from "being wallflowers to rays of sunlight." She asked them if she would get anything special by joining that she couldn't get from the free stuff, and they said absolutely. She didn't have to take their word for it, because she had seen them blossom right in front of her eyes. She'd seen everything blow up for them in a good way. She knew them as shy medical students and she saw what they'd become. And she was just in the right frame of mind, so she went for it.

As soon as she joined, she thought, "Okay, I have some ideas of what I want to do." But in her very first meeting, she was asked about the revenue in her practice, and she had no idea what the revenue was. All she had been worried about was, "Is there enough to pay myself and the people who work with me?"

So her first challenge was to look at her finances. She compares her practice to a plant she had ignored, instead of watering it and nurturing it so it could become something big and beautiful.

In her first seven months with EBS, she went from dabbling to seeing herself as a business owner. She started looking seriously at the money that was coming in and going out. Previously, she had been timid about her practice. She hid from her community. When she hired someone else to join her, they couldn't fill that person's schedule.

In EBS, she learned about putting herself out there and being confident, so she did that and things exploded. She built a team. They connected with a lot of mental health people in the community. She discovered that there were so many people who needed what she provided, but they didn't know about her because she'd been hiding for so long.

Things exploded so much that she was completely overwhelmed. She and her team couldn't keep up with all the referrals and invitations they were getting. "Things got out of control and created a new problem," she says, and that problem was having to hire new people to help them manage all their business needs within the practice.

She can't even imagine what might happen in the next seven months. She finally sees herself on the pathway of her practice someday being an income source without her even working there.

She says her practice is still a work in progress, not perfect by any standards, but she knows that EBS has played such a huge role in her personal growth, in the growth of her practice, and in her ability to deliver the care her community needs. It has positioned her to pursue so many other opportunities, not just within medicine, but consultations, speaking engagements, and more.

"At the end of the day, money is money," Dr. Bolanle says. "When it's sitting in my account, it's not doing anything for me. So using money to invest in myself and my personal development has been amazing for me." She encourages everyone to consider it, especially those who have never invested in growing themselves as business owners and entrepreneurs.

Beyond just seeing patients every day, she's developed other skill sets in EBS that she's been able to flex in so many other ways. "My only regret," she says, "is that I waited so long to join." She followed me from the sidelines for so many years as a self-proclaimed skeptic, thinking she could just figure out a way to be successful on her own.

"I thought I could just do it myself," she says, "but the thing about EBS is that you've got this community of people on the same pathway doing the same things and working hard together. The network here is mind-blowing. If you think of anything you want to do, there's going to be someone in EBS who has resources and connections that can help you get set up to do that. I think that's one of the biggest powers of EBS."

Meet the Doctor Who Started Her Practice with 350 Patients on Her Waitlist

Dr. Karen Kaufman is an allergist/immunologist in northern Virginia. She helps children and adults who suffer from allergies and recurrent infections feel better again and regain the quality of life they deserve. And she's an EBS-for-lifer.

Dr. Karen did her training and fellowship while in the Navy where she spent 10 years on active duty. She joined a multi-specialist group practice and took over as the only allergist. She thought it would be this amazing experience but it led to burnout (at a time when no one was really talking about burnout). And physicians weren't really connecting in the way they connect now. There wasn't a wealth of podcasts. There wasn't much in the way of an online community. So, bit by bit, she had to figure it out by herself. She decided to leave the group practice after 4.5 years and open her own practice.

She got excited about doing this, and then the pandemic hit, and everything got turned upside down. Conferences started going virtual. Spring 2020 was her first introduction to me. I was speaking on thriving in private practice and marketing, and Dr. Karen thought it was "absolutely genius."

"She needs to be my person," she told herself. "I'm going to find her."

That was right around the time the EntreMD podcast was starting. Dr. Karen binge-listened to the podcast in the car on the way to vacation with her family. She told her husband,

"You're going to think I'm crazy, but I think I need to hire a business coach."

I had been practicing for 10 years longer than her, so she wanted to do everything I was doing. She knew she didn't want to reinvent the wheel that had been rolling in a very successful way for me for 10 years. She decided to join EBS in our second cohort in September 2020.

At that time, the majority of the people in EBS weren't in private practice, and she asked me, "How will this apply to private practice?"

I told her about a physician who had a waitlist by doing things they learned in EBS. She hadn't even thought that was possible and got really excited. From September to November 2020, she started marketing herself. *Herself,* not her *business.* She couldn't market her business yet because she was still employed at the other practice.

By the end of January 2021, she had a waitlist of 350 patients who all wanted appointments. She told people they would register them and schedule them before the practice even opened. It all sounded great, until she realized somebody had to call all of these people and set up appointments.

She and her husband and her parents and a couple staff ended up doing it. They got 270 of those patients on the schedule, saw 16 patients on day 1 and they've been booked solid ever since.

The growth was so rapid that there was a lot of troubleshooting, because she ran into problems that brand new business owners don't typically have at that point. Thankfully, the patients didn't know the difference. The practice grew quickly and was serving their community in so many ways.

By the end of the first year, she had not only paid back all the start-up money she had borrowed, but she made more than she did in her fifth year of working as an employed physician.

So year one was a giant success, and she went into year two, trying to get out of the role of constantly being the troubleshooter. At that time, she really went into a period of significant personal growth and growth in mindset. EBS had so much to do with that as she attended some of the live events and connected with colleagues in person. She was challenged to think bigger than she could by herself. She read 20 books in her second year, and she can't remember the last time she had read a single personal development book before that. It was a substantial time of growth.

In March 2022, they registered their 2000th patient, and just nine months later, they had registered their 3000th patient.

What a fantastic year.

By the end of 2022, she was ready to start considering scaling. In October 2022, EBS Scale opened up for people just like her. We were encountering all of these challenges that happen when you start a business and when you market like crazy and do all of the things you learn in EBS, and it was a whole new problem set you have to learn how to navigate.

Her Q4 goal for 2022 was to set the groundwork for growing her team. By February 2023, she had hired a physician and a nurse practitioner. Her team had grown in the office, and they had become a lot more organized and streamlined and everyone was working off of standard operating procedures (SOPs). Everything just got really slick in 2023, and it was a time of amplified growth. Every day she's learning more about scaling and what it takes to hire and grow a team and thrive.

"The EBS gold keeps appearing," she says. "Any time I get great coaching and great guidance, I always circle back on it. I talk about it with my EBS colleagues." She'll listen and re-listen to coaching calls to squeeze every ounce of wisdom out of them.

Dr. Karen now has about 4500 patients. She's been honored repeatedly in her region, not only as a top doctor, but as the face of allergy and immunology. She gets really emotional when she thinks about it.

She's serving her community beyond her wildest dreams. She's being recognized as someone who does that and does it well. Not only is she serving her community, but she's doing it on her own terms.

Her office is just a seven-minute drive from her house. The only downside of that, she says, is less time to listen to the EntreMD podcast. This past summer her son's baseball schedule was uncertain, but her patients were so flexible, and her staff took care of everything. She took a vacation that first year, and all of her patients were like "Good for you!" She's been much more present for her family and friends. She feels so much more connected to people.

And she's been able to serve her community in ways beyond her practice. Her office sponsors the Little League and Youth Football and an organization that brings resources and aid to women in shelters. She loves the community engagement.

She's living her dream life. She has her dream business. And the best part—she's profitable on top of it! It's opening even more doors than she knew she wanted, more doors have opened for her to serve at a greater scale.

What would Dr. Kaufman say to someone who's considering joining the EntreMD Business School?

"Especially for those of us who are in private practice, there's this inner joy in serving people. It is the most freeing way to do it. Entrepreneurship is a hard grind, but it's a very unique role. Entrepreneurs feel each other, because there's a unique skill set we have to develop. Without EBS, I would not have known what the tools were that I truly needed.

By implementing the things I learned, so many things happened. Not only did I build this waitlist, which was awesome, but now, not only am I the face of allergy and immunology for the greater Washington DC area in a magazine, but I'm also the go-to person in every community group I'm in for allergy and immunology. The ability to become a household name is more than I ever dreamed of in business. The only reason I wouldn't join EBS is if you know it all."

Dr. Karen is inspiring, yes, but she's no more of a unicorn than you.

The EntreMD Business School

You've seen examples of what is possible. True examples. We made up Dr. Ebony, but her story is so similar, right? It is possible for you. Please don't buy into the lie that it's not. You've already defied the odds. The average acceptance rate into medical school is 7%. You already did that. You've defied the odds before. You can do this too.

Let Me Tell You More About the EntreMD Business School

EBS is the only school of its kind for physicians who want to build profitable 6-, 7-, and multiple 7-figure businesses. It's a 12-month program with options to level up at the end of the year. This school has been in existence for four years at this point, and what you're about to read are things that have already been accomplished by our students.

The EntreMD Business School will provide the mentorship, accountability, and community you need to:

- **Attract new clients** (articulating what you do, building a referral base, embracing speaking, rocking social media even if you're an introvert or private person)

- **Generate revenue** (understanding your numbers, having those meetings with your biller, understanding revenue generating activities, understanding how to build an efficient workflow, no longer being deceived by billers or equipment sales people or accountants)

- **Build and lead an A team** (How do I find them? How do I lead them? How do I get the best out of them? How do I inspire them?)

- **Build your dream life** (we build businesses and dream lives concurrently)

Like I've said, I've given up the mindset of convincing people to buy what I have to sell. And I encourage you to give it up too. I don't want to convince anybody to join the EntreMD Business School. I want us to give up the idea that sales is this thing where we strong-arm people to buy something they may or may not need.

Selling is not about convincing people *at all*. Rather than trying to convince people to buy something, help people *get what they want*.

For instance, what does a physician with a private practice want? They want a practice where they're able to serve their patients, build and serve a great team, and have a great work environment. And they want to do that in a profitable way, because they understand that it's "no margin, no mission." If I'm not profitable, I can't keep the lights on, I can't make payroll, I have to shut down my practice.

Essentially, they want to be able to *serve* and they want to be able to *earn*.

They would love to be able to create financial freedom so they can serve their patients without worrying about money. They want to be free to do what they want to do with their patients. They want to have time freedom, and they need to build a team in order for that to happen.

For some people, maybe they want to work four days a week or three days a week, and they want to spend time with their family or travel. Maybe they want to work five days a week but they want to be able to take a nice vacation twice a year. They want to be in a position where they're not working when they're at home. They have enough time for their family. They have enough time for their friends, for causes that matter to them. That's really what they want.

So my job as somebody who serves physicians is to help the physicians get what they want. It's not about me selling what I want to sell. It's about me helping them get what they want.

Five Ways I Help People Get What They Want

When I find the right people, those things will be one and the same. Here are five ways I help people get what they want:

#1: Show them what is possible by teaching

#2: Show them what is possible through storytelling

#3: Give them an invitation

#4: Tell them that I understand their fears.

#5: Help them make a decision.

Let's walk through each of these one at a time.

In this book, I've shown you what is possible by teaching. I understand that we're in a time where people think that private practice is dead. I understand that some people have tried it and have gone into serious debt or had to work second jobs to make payroll. If they don't understand business principles, they're at risk of going under.

I've shown you seven simple ways private practice owners are leaving money on the table every single day. I've shown you how to get that money back and what your life could look like when you do.

And I've shown you what is possible by storytelling. I shared a made-up, but very realistic, story about Dr. Ebony, as well as real-life physicians who are living their dream lives and practicing medicine on their terms.

Then I gave you an invitation. I told you that you could do this by yourself, if you want, but some people want mentorship, accountability, and community. Those things exist in a place called the EntreMD Business School, where you'll be surrounded by people who are doing the exact things you want to do. If that's something you want and need, come join us.

I understand your fears, your questions and concerns. I've had them myself and, to be honest, they still float up from time to time. I've just done it for so long that I recognize it for what it is—fear—and I don't let it stop me.

Let's talk about a few of those questions/fears.

Do I have the time to do this? If you think you don't have the time to work on your business, you're right. You don't *have* the time, because you need to learn how to *create* the time. And that's something we teach in the EntreMD Business School. If you don't work on your business, your business doesn't work.

Is this the right time? If you want the truth, the right time was five years ago, so right now is the next best right time. Private practices are going out of business almost every single day. This is a serious thing. If you want to thrive as a private practice owner, you need to figure this stuff out right now. When I was younger, I would say that ignorance is bliss. But ignorance is not bliss as an entrepreneur. It's expensive. It costs money to be ignorant as an entrepreneur.

Do I have the money to do this? Will it be worth my investment? We just finished looking at seven ways you're leaving multiple six figures on the table and how to recoup it. You can figure out how to pay for this. You might have a six-figure tax bill. Are you going to give all that to Uncle Sam, or are you going to take a fraction of it to join the school, invest in yourself, and take a deduction?

Time after time, I have chosen the path of investing in myself, and not once have I ever regretted it.

There Are Only Two Possible Decisions Here

And, finally, because I love people and want to help them get what they want, I help you make a decision. It's not helping you make a decision to join the EntreMD Business School. It's helping you make a decision *period*.

Decision #1: I've thought about it. I don't need what the EntreMD Business School has to offer. I don't need the mentorship. My business is working. I'm already doing all of these things. I don't need accountability, and I definitely do not want any community.

Decision #2: Oh my goodness, this is what I've been looking for. I need this. I'm not entirely sure how this will play out, but I'm committed to my results, and I want to take a chance on myself. I want to get a business education. I want to be in a community with other physician entrepreneurs. I want to be in a community with people who believe in my dreams, people who have done what I want to do so I can watch them. I want to have access to all of these resources. So I'm going to do it.

I want to help people come to "absolutely not" or "absolutely." Indecision is the worst place to be, and I don't want you to stay there, so I'm here to help you get out. I had a mentor who would say that indecision is the worst form of self-abuse. Nothing happens in indecision. Indecision is just hanging in limbo. It's the decision first, and then things start happening.

Whatever you decide, I know I've served you well in the pages of this book. I'm serving the people who decided to work with me, and I've served the people who don't decide to work with me. I'm good with that, because I know that the physician community will be so much better for it. I know the ripple effect will touch tens of thousands of people, starting from this moment. So that's a gift.

I know that a percentage of people will say yes, the EntreMD Business School is the best next step for me. When we built EBS, we weren't looking to create a traditional school. We were looking to support physicians on their journey. So what did we do? We built in mentorship, accountability, and community. That's what I need to thrive as an entrepreneur. That's what you need to thrive as an entrepreneur.

It's a container, so you can continue to acquire and refine the skills that you need in order to get the results you want, so you can practice medicine and live life on your terms. When you join EBS, I'll have the privilege of working with you for at least a year in a container where we'll make the things we talked about in this book a reality.

And I know that we'll create magic together.

We're not in a space where we have to spend our energy convincing people to join us because we have a community that is unrivaled. It's unbelievable how amazing the physicians are. These are elite physicians who are building these great businesses and getting great results. The connections are so powerful, and the way they look out for each other and root for each other is unparalleled.

It's a safe place where people who are having challenges can come and say, "Oh my goodness, this is so hard," and people come out to support. Someone else might say, "We just crossed a million dollars in revenue!" and people come out and support them too. It's amazing.

We've got people enrolled in EBS who are just starting out, people doing $8 million in business, and everyone in between. We've got the whole gamut there. People who are starting a business are hungry and on fire. When you've been at this for a while, you start to settle, you start to cruise, you're on autopilot, and sometimes you just need a fresh burst of inspiration and energy.

On the flip side, the veteran business owners are showing the younger people what is possible. It's a space of beautiful mutuality, with everyone learning from each other and inspiring each other.

We're not trying to convince people to join, because we only want people who want to be in a space like that. We want people who will add to our culture and enhance it. When new doctors come in, I think, "Man, they're going to be such a gift to the community, and the community is going to be such a gift to them." It's a two-way street.

You serve everybody, and then you serve your clients at the highest level. You can do it all day every day. I get to do what I love to do—serve. Since I'm serving, I can sell ethically and authentically and with integrity. The community will be better for it, your clients will be better for it, your business will be better for it.

It's a win-win-win situation, friends. It really truly is.

To get more details and apply to the EntreMD Business School, go here www.entremd.com/business.

Final Words From Me To You

In 2016 it dawned on me that, if my only skill was doctoring, I was going to be in trouble. Eight years ago, no one believed me. When I would post about that in Facebook groups, I would get dragged. People thought I was crazy. It didn't make sense, but I knew it in my bones. I knew that whatever was coming was not good.

Now it makes perfect sense. No one thinks I'm crazy these days. They recognize my feelings from eight years ago as intuition and foresight. And because of that intuition and foresight, my practice grew during the COVID-19 pandemic. I've built it as a sellable entity. I launched EntreMD. I have a podcast and we're at over 650,000 downloads. I've written three best-selling books and founded the EntreMD Business School. And I've been on a sabbatical for the past two years.

All of that came out of taking a chance on myself, saying yes, and believing I would figure it out as I went. I asked myself: how can I make this possible? Not only that, but what is possible that I can't even imagine right now?

The gift you can give yourself today is the gift of a decision. Absolutely I'm doing this or absolutely this is not for me. That middle place? That indecisiveness? Is where dreams go to die.

When you decided to go to medical school, you took out six figures in loans and gave up a decade of your life. You made a decision and you acted on it. There's no way you accidentally wait and become a physician.

And there's no way you're going to accidentally stumble upon your dream life. You're going to make decisions that will get you there.

I'm at this stage in my life where I venture into the unknown very confidently because it's magic on the other side. There's no way I could have known that my life would look the way it looks now. No way. But, one day, five years ago, I was just like you, and I had an opportunity to make a decision.

Remember—this is about *you* and your dream. It's about what *you* want your life and business to look like. There are so many physicians out there living their dream lives and practicing medicine on their terms, and there is *no* reason at all why you can't do the very same thing.

I've given you a whole lot to think about in this book, but I've also made it perfectly clear: the EntreMD Business School helps physicians make their dreams a reality. Those are just the facts.

I can't possibly express to you how deep and rich and impactful this community is until you've been immersed in it and experienced it for yourself.

It will change your life.

It has been an absolute gift to have the opportunity to help thousands of doctors live their dream lives and practice medicine on their own terms.

I'd love for you to join us. We'll see you on the inside.

Acknowledgments

I want to thank the following special people:

Makeda Omensa, who runs so much behind the scenes in all my businesses and in my life. Thank you for doing all you do so I have the freedom to live nine lives at once.

Fatima Sparks, my practice administrator who has led our practice through a pandemic, the great resignation and hyperinflation. Without your work, I would not be free to change the lives of tens of thousands of physicians.

The physicians of the EntreMD Business School. You are the ones building the most innovative, most impactful and most profitable businesses inside and outside healthcare. Working with you is one of the greatest honors of my life. I am grateful for you beyond words.

Steve Unachukwu, my husband who gives me the gift of inspiration, belief and accountability so I can defy the status quo every single day.

My four children, Cheta, Chidi, Chichi and Esther. I love you so much and I am so proud of you. You make me infinitely better than I could have ever been without you.

About the Author

Dr. Nneka Unachukwu helps physicians build profitable 7 and 7+ figure businesses by teaching them the simple, proven and timeless principles used by the ultra successful. She knows that entrepreneurship is a vehicle physicians can leverage so they can have the freedom to live life and practice medicine on their terms. She does this through the EntreMD Business School, the only school of its kind for physician entrepreneurs, the EntreMD podcast, a top 1% podcast, and her best-selling books.

Before starting EntreMD, Dr. Una started her own pediatric private practice, a practice she still runs fourteen years later. In her typical unconventional fashion, she built it as a true business, one that can run efficiently and profitably without her involvement in the day-to-day management.

Dr. Una has been featured in *Forbes* and her company has been on the Inc. 5000 list of fastest-growing privately held companies in America for two years in a row.

She resides outside Atlanta with her husband and four children.

Connect with Dr. Una

Podcast
www.entremd.com/podcast

Website
www.EntreMD.com

YouTube
@drunachukwu

Facebook
@drunachukwu

Private Facebook Community
EntreMD - Physicians in Business

LinkedIn
@druna

Instagram
@drunachukwu

Made in the USA
Middletown, DE
13 August 2024

59036974R00075